WHAT DO YOU
SAY WHEN...

What do you say when...

Talking to people
with confidence

on any

Social or business
occasion

F L O R E N C E   I S A A C S

CLARKSON POTTER/PUBLISHERS
NEW YORK

CLARKSON POTTER is a trademark and POTTER
with colophon is a registered trademark of Random House, Inc.

Library of Congress Cataloging-in-Publication Data
Isaacs, Florence.
    What do you say when— / Florence Isaacs. — 1st ed.
        p.   cm.
    1. Conversation.   2. Oral communication.   3. Etiquette.   I. Title.
    BJ2121.I83   2009
    395—dc22   2008040535

ISBN 978-0-307-40528-9

Printed in the United States of America

Design by Dominika Dmytrowski

10   9   8   7   6   5   4   3   2   1

First Edition

ACKNOWLEDGMENTS

My old friend Jimmy Viera was my muse for this book. Jimmy has changed my life at least twice (so far).

Crucial help also came from Martha Halperin and Maurice Leon; my sister Roberta Satow, Ph.D.; Barbara Reilly; Denise Dorman; Sander A. Flaum; Loren Weybright; Chris Adamec; Sally Wendkos Olds; Irene S. Levine, Ph.D.; Anne Hart; Hollis Brooks; Suzanne Bates; and Mary Hogan, author of *Pretty Face.*

For their insights, I thank dating expert Ian Coburn, author of *God Is a Woman: Dating Disasters;* Paul Marciano, Ph.D.; Karin Sterling Anderson, coauthor of *Finding Your Mate Online;* Patti Wood; Susan Bulkeley Butler; Louis Lautman; Michelle Tillis Lederman; and Mark Scott. Valuable aid was also provided by Barbara Safani; Buddy Howard; Shel Horowitz; Joanne Feierman; Michael Cummings; Andrea Nierenberg; John K. Gillespie, Ph.D.; Wendy L. Kinney; Paul Schaye; Ronnie Moore; Charlene Langer, Art Institute of Pittsburgh; Lauren Swann, M.S., R.D., L.D.N.; Jeff Coppersmith; Harold Brauner; Jerome Levine, M.D.; and Susan Behrens, Ph.D.

I thank my agent and friend Linda Konner, who encouraged me to revisit an idea I had dropped—and then ran with this project. Without Linda, *What Do You Say When...* would still be a thin file in my office drawer.

CONTENTS

INTRODUCTION

Have you ever felt anxious or uncertain at a social or business event filled with fifty (or one hundred or two hundred) chattering people? Have you dreaded attending a dinner party or a wedding where you knew few guests (or none at all)? Yes, there are some people who dive into such situations with supreme confidence and may even look forward to them. Rather than feel intimidated, they seem to thrive on meeting new people. They know just what to say and when to say it, whether at a cocktail party, a conference, or a Fourth of July barbecue. There are others, however, who have to work hard to acquire conversation skills and self-confidence. I am one of them.

Like many people, I did not emerge from the womb with a sparkling personality. I grew up shy and unsure of myself, a borderline introvert who clung to the corners. In college I sat in the last row of every class, hiding and hoping I'd never be called upon. Entering the student lounge alone amounted to an act of courage. My stomach knotted; my palms perspired. What if nobody talked to me? I'd look as if I had no friends in a room where everyone else seemed to belong. These fears led to a conscious effort to learn how to smoke at that time. A cigarette dangling from my fingers made me look like a sophisticate, I thought, and gave me something to do with my hands.

Later on, after I landed my first job, I decided to try another approach. I happened to read a newspaper article on the art of conversation, and thought, "I can do that." I tried the suggestions one by one, and very gradually began to sharpen my skills. People started to mention how easy it was to talk to me, fueling my confidence. My social and professional relationships slowly multiplied and flourished.

During this process, I learned that with determination and practice, it is possible to talk with people on any occasion and in any setting, even if it doesn't come naturally at first. It is also possible to develop charm and poise you never knew you possessed. I know this is true because I've done it myself.

With motivation and the right tools, you can grow more self-assured and learn to establish meaningful connections with people you may or may not know. You can have more fun and become someone others enjoy being around and therefore seek out.

If that goal seems impossible at this moment, try to suspend your doubts for just a while. In the course of writing this book, I have interviewed many people, including psychotherapists, business and personal coaches, individuals who must socialize as part of their job, and ordinary people who are simply good at meeting and talking to others. During our conversations, many have confessed, "I'm basically shy," or "I'm a learned extrovert. I just force myself to do these things." They were able to push against an innate personality trait and stretch themselves.

Chances are that with the right mind-set you can stretch, too. If you're like most people, you can enhance your conversation skills and grow more at ease with others. Ironically, one of the most important skills involves not talking at all, but knowing how and when to keep quiet and listen. Some very smart, talented people fall short in this area, to the detriment of career advancement and/or social acceptance.

You can learn how to circulate on any occasion, drawing

on any number of appropriate conversation topics, and how to keep conversation moving comfortably in one-on-one situations. "For me, the worst is meeting and talking to a new client for the first time—and figuring out what to say after the introductions," an advertising account executive told me. It becomes easier to make such transitions when you start thinking in new ways.

An architect needed help talking to people he's just met for another reason. "I go to a party, say things I shouldn't, and wind up in arguments about politics," he lamented. There are ways to handle hot-button issues without getting into trouble and to turn them into meaningful interchanges.

It's never been more important to develop your conversation skills than it is right now in the age of quick, constant communication—and also shallow, sometimes mindless chatter. Technology has revolutionized how, when, and how fast we contact one another. Yet cell phones and computers do not suffice to build relationships, and they have eroded social skills. Years ago, people didn't check e-mail during restaurant dinners.

The core of communication is face-to-face. You don't build trust or convey important ideas in a text message. You don't seal a deal, make an indelible impression, or charm someone electronically. Ultimately you meet with people in person to interview for a job or to date. Cell phones may have become fixtures in our lives, but they won't help you have a good time at someone's engagement party, meet people at a chamber of commerce event, schmooze with a client, or hang out with a potential friend. It should come as no surprise that recruiters at graduate business schools rate communication and interpersonal skills at the top of their list of important qualities. These same skills help you advance further and earn more.

At the same time, networking has skyrocketed in importance as people change jobs more often and as more of us become independent contractors and own small businesses. There's also a need for purely social networks to bring support and meaning to our lives. It takes know-how to reach out to others in order to initiate and deepen personal bonds.

You already have resources at your disposal to help you improve your conversation skills. The task is to become aware and use them. Everyone has insecurities. One thing is certain: you aren't going to meet or connect with people unless you're willing to take a chance and move beyond your comfort zone—starting now.

Perhaps the well-known story of the late famed psychotherapist Albert Ellis will inspire you. Painfully shy at age nineteen, Ellis became determined to change. His solution was to sit on a park bench day after day and talk to any woman who sat down. By the end of the month, he had engaged in conversations with almost 130 females. A determined person can overcome almost anything.

HOW TO USE THIS BOOK

Some people love to socialize, and one man attributes his social comfort and confidence to his parents. "They chatted up a storm. I remember sitting in the car as a kid, impatiently waiting for them to finish their conversation," he told me. He also grew up with six siblings who got along with one another. However, if you do not share his background, or even if you do, this book can help.

In order to make this book as useful as possible, I've organized it by type of occasion. Each offers unique opportunities for conversation that you may not have considered before. Before you attend a social or business function, large or small, you can turn to the relevant chapter for issues to consider, effective conversation openers, and other tips on what to say and how to behave. Even if you receive a last-minute invitation, you'll find instant advice that can make the experience more productive and enjoyable.

To get the most out of this book:

1. **Learn the conversation strategies that apply across the board, regardless of the occasion, in Chapters 1 and 2.** Fill out the quiz in Chapter 1 to assess your own strengths and challenges. See Chapter 2 for the basic rules of conversation, including all-purpose topics that fit any person or situation.

2. **Check Chapter 3 for conversation openers and other tips at social events, including cocktail parties, charity benefits, and house/apartment parties.** Chapter 4 covers date-related conversation strategies at bars, parties, and at initial face-to-face meetings with someone you've met online. See Chapter 5 for conversation ideas when hosting a dinner party or when attending one as a guest.

3. **Read Chapter 6 for conversation tips to make holidays and other family get-togethers more enjoyable, meaningful, and relaxed.** Included is advice on how to talk to kids in the family and get more than one-word answers. Because vacations are more fun when you talk to people, see Chapter 7 for conversation starters when traveling abroad, on cruises, at resorts, and more. Don't go to a wedding without reading Chapter 8, whether you're a guest or the bride or groom.

4. **Realize that the conversational issues are different on business and professional occasions.** Check Chapter 9 for conversation strategies at conventions, conferences, trade shows, and meetings. When you want to take a brief professional encounter to the next level and get to know someone better,

read Chapter 10. There you'll learn how to build a bond with a prospective client or a new customer or contact—whether you're in the person's office, dining in a restaurant, or out on the golf course. Chapter 11 gives you an edge at job interviews. It covers all you need to know about answering questions, connecting with the interviewer, and standing out from other candidates.

5. **Approach other situations with special sensitivity.** Chapter 12 tells you just what to say at difficult times such as funerals, health crises, or when someone has been laid off or is going through a divorce. You can teach your children conversation skills to navigate relationships—and life—by using the tips in Chapter 13. Chapter 14 leads you to resources for when you need extra help to strengthen etiquette or other skills.

The information ahead has already helped me to boost my own conversation skills and confidence. My goal now is to help you improve yours.

PART I

LEARNING THE BASICS

Conversation:
Your Entrée Anywhere

Imagine you're seated next to Bill Gates at a dinner. What do you say? How do you strike up a conversation with someone at the pool on vacation? What do you say when you want to approach a contact at a convention or a trade show? You probably have a great deal to say and several ways to open a conversation in any of these scenarios. Yet you may not recognize the options due to common roadblocks that set you up to feel inadequate. To move past these obstacles, you have to be willing to change the way you think about people (and yourself)—and ask some important questions.

THE ANXIETY FACTOR

Anxiety tends to be the biggest block to comfortable conversation because it undermines confidence and makes it impossible to relax. It was anxiety that drained my own sense of self—and if you have trouble interacting on social and business occasions, you probably know anxiety well. One or more of the following scripts may run through your mind:

- I have nothing to talk about.
- No one is interested in talking to me.
- They all know one another.
- I don't know how to start a conversation.
- I'll be rejected.
- I'll run out of things to say.
- I'll say something dumb and look foolish.

Does at least part of this list sound familiar? You may even convince yourself that "I don't want to talk to them anyway. I'd rather go home and walk the dog." Few people totally escape such negative self-talk at times, which feeds insecurity and awkwardness. The scripts can stop you from meeting people, and affect your ability to listen to them when you do. If you're focused on your deficits, it's hard to hear what someone else is saying to you. Maybe the anxiety started when other kids made fun of you at school or a critical parent or teacher embarrassed you. Or perhaps you grew up in a home where there wasn't much relaxed conversation. But you're now an adult and the past is behind you. There is always something to say to people when you start thinking in new directions.

Refocus Your Anxiety

The first step you can take to feel more comfortable is to move the spotlight off yourself and what people think of you, and switch it onto a simple question: "Who can I meet here and what can I learn?" Now you've reframed your fear of rejection or awkwardness into something positive. Instead of panicking when introduced to Bill Gates, you might say something like, "How are you? I've heard so much about your foundation. What are your latest projects?" You've refocused the entire experience and launched a promising interchange. Conversation openers like that, tailored to the individual, begin to flow naturally when you start to think differently and use certain tools.

Maybe you hesitate to initiate conversation at a cocktail reception. What if someone you approach gives you the cold shoulder? Many people build invisible barriers around themselves as a defense against rejection. A reality check can help give you perspective. Rejection happens far less often than you might expect. Chances are the other person feels just as vulnerable as you do when meeting new people and will welcome your approach. If that doesn't happen, you can learn to be less sensitive and simply move on. Not everyone is going to respond to you. So what?

Possibilities for rejection arise in many situations. The issue really is how are you going to handle them? For example, I received an invitation to a communications symposium a while ago. I vacillated about attending because I wasn't sure the program would be relevant enough to my interests. Ultimately, I decided to take a risk and go. When I arrived, I looked around the room and deliberately headed toward a table with just two empty seats. I decided that a crowded table offered more chances to meet interesting people and hear useful information.

I walked over to a chair and asked the person to the left, "May I join you? Is this seat available?" The answer was "No, it isn't." I immediately moved to the other empty chair and repeated the same question to someone else. This time, I got the seat. Years earlier, the same scene would have played out very differently. I'd slink away after the first "no," feeling humiliated. Yet *I* wasn't being rejected. The "no" had nothing at all to do with me. It was about an occupied chair.

To avoid the possibility of rejection, some people always

choose near-empty tables. It has to do with fear of asking for anything. There's always the chance the seat is taken or your neighbor won't want to lend you the lawn mower or the girl already has a date. But if you don't ask, you definitely won't get what you want.

Identifying Your Objective

Another way to refocus your anxiety is to ask yourself, "Why am I here and what do I want from this event or encounter?" The answer helps you decide who you want to talk to and what you want to talk about. The goal at a friend's party may be to meet nice people and have a good time. At a conference, you may want to learn industry news and talk to the keynote speaker. Or you may want to connect with prospective customers. If you're there to network, you may want to meet as many people as you can—or target two or three specifically. When you're hosting a dinner party, your usual goal is to orchestrate an enjoyable evening for guests.

Each occasion offers its own unique possibilities for conversation. At the symposium I attended, everyone discussed business-related topics, of course. But people also chatted about the location (an extraordinary new building) as well as the philanthropist who financed it and the dinner in a historic mansion that would conclude the event that evening.

At other times, you may want to deepen a relationship with an acquaintance. Certain techniques and strategies can help you build a personal connection. There are many paths to conversation when you become alert to them.

As you change your perspective and keep your eye on your goal, you will begin to experience people differently. Instead of viewing them as obstacles or threats, you will see them as opportunities, possibilities, and resources.

PREPARATION AND PLANNING

You will also navigate a social or business function more comfortably and effectively if you do a little homework in advance. For example, perhaps a client has invited you to his daughter's wedding. You can find out who else is going to be there. The more you know about the occasion and the guest list, the more confident and relaxed you're going to feel. You may discover that an acquaintance or two will attend, and you won't be as alone as you thought—or that someone you've always wanted to meet will be there. At your leisure you can figure out what you might talk about with the person. You have a plan.

Appropriate preparation varies, depending on the situation. To give yourself something to talk about with other attendees at an upcoming charity benefit, you can research online the organization's mission and activities. Planning ahead helps you make the most of your time at professional events and feel better at a singles party. Maybe you'd feel more comfortable at the party if you asked a friend to go with you. You don't want to glue yourselves together, which discourages others from approaching you, but a familiar presence can help you feel more secure.

ARMING YOURSELF WITH OPENERS

If your heart starts pounding and your palms perspire at the thought of making the first move, try to view your approach as a series of small steps. First, all you have to do is extend your hand. Introduce yourself with, "Hello, I'm John [or Joyce] Smith. And you are?" Pause for a response. Then ask an open-ended question. This type of question encourages conversation to continue and heads off dead-end "yes" or "no" answers that leave you groping for what to say next. The icebreakers below are polite and work well in most situations:

- "What brings you here?"
- "What do you think about . . . [the new school principal, the pending legislation]?"
- "What's your opinion of . . . [the morning speaker, the new car models]?"
- "Can you recommend . . . [an internist, a deer repellent]?"

Certain targeted statements can also stimulate further interchange, such as:

- "Tell me about . . . [your company, new job, your house or baby]."
- "I want to hear all about . . . [your trip to Bora Bora or the trade deal with XYZ]."
- "Educate me about . . . [windsurfing or your organization]."

Commit these all-purpose conversation openers to memory, ready for use as needed. Eventually, you're likely to come up with others on your own that you can adapt to the person and situation. After listening to the response, you can comment on what has been said to keep conversation rolling and/or ask probing follow-up questions. Years ago, I found myself unexpectedly seated next to former president Jimmy Carter at an awards luncheon honoring Rosalynn Carter. I had no time to prepare, but I managed to tell him, "I'm honored to meet you. You're my first president."

He laughed and turned out to be an enormously charming, attractive man with a sense of humor. I asked him questions like "What do you miss most since leaving the White House?" and "Tell me what you're focusing on now." Open-ended questions and targeted statements can advance conversations and encourage anyone—even presidents—to talk.

TAKE IT SLOW

You're going to find opportunities to meet, learn, and get the results you want all around you, including some unexpected places. It will take time to accustom yourself to this new way of thinking and to resist negative chatter in your head. It does help to acknowledge your fears one by one, which diminishes their power and helps you feel more in control. Then you can start problem solving.

Expect to feel awkward at first. It's part of the process. I had to struggle, too. Although you won't become the life of the party overnight, you're likely to see small improvements pretty quickly.

QUIZ: What Are Your Strengths and Challenges?

Most people have some issues with conversation. To raise your awareness and identify gaps in your own skills, try this self-assessment quiz. Circle the answer that most accurately applies to you.

1. When I enter a room full of strangers at a social or business event, I
   a. hope someone talks to me.
   b. look for someone who is also alone and introduce myself.
   c. stand next to a group of people talking to one another.

2. When conversing with someone I've just met or barely know, I
   a. try to be entertaining.
   b. talk mostly about myself.
   c. draw the person out and encourage him/her to talk.

3. When I meet someone new, I'm likely to talk about
   a. the weather.
   b. politics or religion.
   c. topics related to the event I'm attending.

4. When I don't know guests at a wedding or dinner party, I
   a. worry what to say to people at my table.
   b. talk to table mates about the bride and groom or the location.
   c. sit quietly and watch guests dance.

5. When I speak to people, I
   a. make eye contact.
   b. bend my head down.
   c. glance around the room.

6. When I want to exit a conversation and move on to someone else at a reception, I
   a. shuffle my feet and search for a chance to leave.
   b. say, "Nice meeting you," and walk away.
   c. say, "I must say hello to Bill, but I really enjoyed talking to you."

7. At social and business events, I
   a. keep a neutral expression on my face.
   b. look bored if that's how I feel.
   c. smile frequently.

8. If someone seems uninterested in a topic I've raised, I
   a. switch to another subject or move on to someone else.
   b. wonder what to do.
   c. keep talking.

9. If I'm chatting with people and notice someone nearby who seems to want to join us, I
   a. glance over and wonder who he/she is.
   b. invite the person into the group.
   c. continue talking and ignore the person.

10. When there's a momentary pause in conversation, I
   a. feel uncomfortable.
   b. use the time to think about what's been said.
   c. immediately talk about anything, just to fill the silence.

CORRECT ANSWERS

1: **B.** It's hard to be proactive, but the goal is to try to stretch your comfort zone and take a chance, rather than stand on the sidelines.

2: **C.** People love to talk about themselves, and will love to talk to you when you listen and show you're interested.

3: **C.** The weather is boring, and it's a good idea to avoid controversial issues like politics and religion.

4: **B.** It's a guest's responsibility to participate in the occasion and chat with people.

5: **A.** Eye contact is essential to conversation because it connects you to people and signals that they have your full attention.

6: **C.** Nobody wants to feel stuck, but you can exit gracefully and leave people feeling good about your talk.

7: **C.** People think you're unfriendly or angry or unhappy to be there if you don't smile—and they're less likely to approach you.

8: **A.** Read others' signals and be flexible. You don't want to bore people.

9: **B.** You may learn something from the person, and it's smart to be inclusive.

10: **B.** Everyone needs to take a breath at times. Don't let anxiety take over.

If you chose most of these correct answers, you seem able to approach people and handle conversation well in common situations. Keep it up, and become even better at the art of conversation with the tips and strategies that follow.

If you answered differently, you may be discouraging people from initiating conversation with you, or even pushing them away without realizing it. The purpose of this quiz is to stimulate thinking about your conversation skills and to pinpoint areas that need work. You may also want to ask a trusted friend for an opinion of how you come across and specific trouble spots. In the chapters ahead, you'll learn how to make changes and apply new skills to help you socially and professionally.

②

FOLLOW THE RULES

Years ago I attended a press conference where a nationally known journalist asked some piercing questions. As the session ended, I found myself filing out of the room right beside her. "You did a great job up there," I said. To my surprise, her face lit up with pleasure. "Thank you so much," she replied. "I never hear that from colleagues."

It was clear she genuinely appreciated my words, and I learned something important that day. I learned that the high and mighty, the rich and famous, and the powerful can feel just as insecure as you and me. And they respond to sincere admiration. I didn't realize it at the time, but I had used one of the rules of conversation—and made a contact.

The rules I'm talking about are my own general guidelines for conversation. The rules help equip you to talk to anyone on any occasion and feel more confident.

TEN RULES THAT WORK

Perhaps you already abide by some of these rules unknowingly; perhaps not. Some may come more easily to you than others.

Regardless, they help stimulate ideas and lead to paths of conversation that may not have occurred to you before. Experience the benefits when you follow the following rules.

1. Find Out What You Have In Common

"We tend to be drawn to and interact with others from similar educational, economic, racial, and ethnic backgrounds because we're comfortable with people like us. In the academic world it's called the homophily principle," says Jeanne S. Hurlbert, Ph.D., professor of sociology at Louisiana State University. "Although differences can spice up relationships, similarity is a surer path to close relationships."

The fact is, if you and someone you just met at a professional event or a party grew up in the same town or city and/or attended the same college, you have an instant opening for conversation. You've had similar experiences that make you feel connected. You may know some of the same people. The next time you meet, you can pick up where you left off. This is a tremendous advantage when you want to develop business as well as social relationships.

If you're from a completely different background (or maybe even another country), the notion of what you have in common has to broaden. The task is to look for other points of connection: maybe you both have children of the same age or you share important interests. If you both love books on politics, or are stamp collectors, film fans, racquetball players, or art or opera lovers, you have a lot to talk about. At a social function you may discover you and another guest are both database administrators or fundraisers. Or you can always talk shop or ask an open-ended question like "What are your biggest problems with . . . ?"

2. Focus on the Other Person

An attorney tells the story of meeting a former law school class-mate and asking, "How have you been?" The classmate proceeded to describe in detail every minute spent since the day he graduated fifteen years earlier; he did not understand the concept of boundaries and limits or the true meaning of conversation.

A conversation is not a monologue. It's a verbal exchange. The idea is to invite in the other person, not talk endlessly about yourself (or anything else). I once met someone at a party who kept chattering about computer technology. I asked a simple question about my printer and he told me more than I ever wanted to know. He left me thinking, "When does he come up for air?"

In contrast, people think you're a fascinating conversationalist when you encourage them to talk about themselves and their interests. This is true regardless of whether you're on the beach, at a family reunion, or at an industry convention. If a prospective customer tells you he just went kayaking for the first time and loved it, don't just respond, "Oh," and leave it at that. Follow up and use his statement as a springboard for more questions and more conversation. Say, "Tell me about the sport," and he'll be your best friend (and you'll get educated, too). Did you realize that kayaks are far more environmentally friendly than motor boats? Now you do.

3. Listen Up

It sounds quite simple, but good listeners can be hard to find. Due to anxiety, insensitivity, or other factors, some people talk too much or have difficulty focusing on what someone else is saying.

Active listening is an effective way to listen and respond. You give your full attention to the other person and signal that you are listening via eye contact, nodding, smiling, or laughing in appropriate places, and saying "Uh huh," "Yes," "I see," and so forth, to encourage the person to continue. If you're listening to a sad story, a sincere, well-timed "Oh my goodness" communicates your empathy. To head off misunderstandings, you can also paraphrase what you believe the person has said, as in, "So you're upset with the workmanship." This kind of statement gives the person a chance to repeat or explain further, if necessary.

Active listening tells people that you are tuned in to their concerns. It helps you understand their point of view, focus on what they want, need, and feel, and is essential to deepening relationships. But it takes practice. I was fortunate enough to learn how to do it through volunteer work on two crisis hotlines over the years.

Corporations sometimes send key employees to intensive courses in listening. You can't work productively with colleagues or learn what a client's challenges are unless you keep quiet and listen. A successful executive recalls that a mentor once told him, "You're very smart, but you've got to work on your listening skills. Before I tell you what the problem is, you seem to have an answer. But your answer is sometimes wrong because you haven't listened to the whole problem."

It's a human impulse to interrupt and to make assumptions, but that can annoy people—and hurt you. For example, if you keep interrupting someone giving you directions to the mall, you might not reach your destination.

Realize, too, that at times silence is part of conversation. The ability to pause and consider what you think and feel (and to let the other person do the same) allows space. It's a sign of comfort with each other. However, many people have trouble tolerating silence. Their discomfort can lead them to rush to fill the void—and that's when they're most likely to say something inappropriate. People like you when you hear and understand what they are saying.

4. Join the "Compliment Club"

Like the journalist I spoke to at the press conference, people bask in the glow of approval. They love hearing praise for their accomplishment, performance, or sense of humor. They're flattered when their good taste is appreciated. Compliments are guaranteed conversation starters whether you're talking to a stranger or someone you already know. You can always try something like one of these statements:

- "What a beautiful tie."
- "That's a handsome briefcase."
- "Your comments at the meeting were right on the mark."
- "I always look forward to seeing you."
- "I admire your . . . [dedication, honesty, style]."
- "What a great idea."
- "What an excellent parent [or nurse, etc.] you are."

These words affirm and assure the person "I want to be friendly. I'm *for* you." A compliment encourages further conversation because it tells people they're special, makes them feel good, and implies "I'm really interested in talking to you." There is almost always something positive you can find to say. On the other hand, make your praise genuine. Don't fib that you love someone's jokes when they really make you wince. Sooner or later, the truth always comes out.

There are times when you may feel a compliment is expected from you, yet praise would be dishonest. Perhaps an acquaintance is interviewed on TV, and the result is less than impressive. You might try a creative response, such as "I saw you on CNN. Congratulations!" The words are positive. You're telling the truth, and everybody's happy. You did not say, "You were awesome."

5. Build an Inventory of Talk Topics

There are times when you don't share natural or comfortable points of commonality with someone. What do you say to the Dalai Lama? What do you say to a chess champion if you never played the game, or a nuclear physicist? If you know in advance the person will attend the same event, don't expect to talk off the cuff. Think about possible conversation tracks, and ask a friend for suggestions. When you try to "wing it," you set yourself up for long, uncomfortable silences and inappropriate blurts. Instead, turn to a reservoir of subjects you can draw upon almost anytime:

Sports. Talk about basketball, football, tennis, golf, cyclist Lance Armstrong, or the Olympics. (If you don't know hockey but do know baseball, mention that.) Glance at the sports pages of the newspaper to keep up to date. Just the headlines can help you stay topical. You don't have to be an expert on football, but you should be able to chat a bit.

If you're seated next to the president of the United States at a White House dinner, the closest you should get to politics is a congressman's loud ties. But you can talk about workout routines or the White House gym. Sports are also a good topic when speaking with international visitors. You might ask, "What are the most popular sports in [name of country]?"

Finance. Today, taxes, real estate, and the stock market are universal subjects just like sports—even more so because more women are likely to be interested. Be careful about divulging personal information, however. Remember to talk about pension changes or insurance costs in general, never about your own finances. Put it this way: "I heard the mortgage rate is up again," not "I just got this five percent mortgage."

Entertainment. This category breaks down to films, TV, theater, books, and concerts. You can say, "I saw . . . [or read/attended . . .]" or "I want to see . . . [or read/attend . . .]." Be sure to ask about shows or books the other person has seen or read. Be aware of current popular TV shows. Even if you watch only the news, you can check the entertainment section of the newspaper to stay updated on new series that are creating buzz or old ones that are close to conclusion and keeping everyone guessing.

Fashion. You may think this is a topic only for women, but you'd be wrong. Men pick out ties to match their shirts and then some.

Children. If you know the person is a parent, you can always talk about how the kids are doing, their school or summer camp. This advice applies whether you're chatting with your third cousin, the CEO of a Fortune 500 company, a movie star, or the Norwegian ambassador. In the latter case, you can also talk about the envoy's country, as in, "I've never been to Norway. Tell me about it," or "I spent two days in Oslo several years ago. Have there been many changes?"

The Venue. Are you attending a benefit for a concert hall? You can discuss the hall's new sound system or the current performance schedule. At a university conference, try something like, "What do you think of the new campus?" or "Did you know this is one of the most diverse schools in the country?"

Health and Wellness News. The latest report on cholesterol or the top story about a newfangled diet also grabs people's attention. Just stick to "What do you think about . . . ?" to move the conversation along. Food and travel are also topics of broad interest that can be explored.

6. Know When to Receive Information

If you're out of your depth and don't know what to say about a subject, this is a time to become a recipient of information and admit, "I don't know much about that. Please educate me." This works well when you're introduced to that chess champion.

A friend of mine used a variation when invited to a party attended by a famous scientist. My friend approached the man and said, "I've never met a Nobel Prize winner before. I'm so glad to see you. Can you tell me about your work?" My friend, a fashion industry executive, knew nothing about science and didn't say a word about it. Instead he became a *recipient of information*. The Nobel Prize winner talked to *him* for an hour, which he enjoyed.

In a similar situation, I asked a medical researcher, "What led you to this field? Did you always know this was what you wanted?" He told me, "When I had a tonsillectomy as a child, I was fascinated by the anesthesia. I knew then that I wanted to know how this works."

If you're introduced to the Dalai Lama, you might say to him, "I'm honored to meet you. You've done so much for humanity. How do you manage to keep up with your busy schedule?" If there's time to talk together at length, you might try a more complicated question, such as "What do you consider to be your most important work right now?" Context does matter. You can't expect to have a long, serious conversation on a receiving line.

Sometimes you have to work harder. I once met a research scientist at an engagement party. His work involved complex genetic investigations, so I had to find something else to discuss with him. Through small talk, I learned this man lived only a block away from his research institute. When he had an inspiration at midnight, he could walk right over to his laboratory. I commented on his passion for his work, and the conversation took off. I didn't know much about genetics, but I did know about loving your job.

7. Remember What You Heard Last Time

This book is about talking to people you don't know or don't know well. When conversing with someone you've met before, you already have certain basic information. You can greet the person with "Nice to see you again," and refer to something the person said the last time, as in "I've been thinking about what you told me about XYZ." Or mention information you've heard about the person, as in "I hear you're moving your office across town." Or ask, "How did that deal go?" or "How did the comic book convention [or the art class] turn out?" If you meet someone for the second time and remember to ask, "How are the triplets?" you're going to go far.

8. Know How and When to Talk About Yourself

Conversation is a two-way street, and of course there's a place for you to offer information. When someone inquires, "Are you a stock analyst?" don't just give a one-word answer. Elaborate on questions you're asked to advance conversation. Mention the firm you work for and the types of stocks you follow. This information gives the other person a basis for continuing the conversation.

You may have heard the term "elevator speech," which is a "pitch" that introduces you to someone else in the time it takes to ride a few floors in an elevator—perhaps thirty seconds. The idea is to present the most pertinent information about yourself (relative to the situation) very quickly. This is no place for arrogance, pretentiousness, or unwarranted claims to importance. There's a difference between telling someone, "I'm the greatest," and giving facts about yourself that speak for themselves, as in "I've been manufacturing widgets for ten years for the Department of Defense and other customers."

Understand what the other person wants out of the conversation. At a cocktail party, it isn't your life history. Even at a job interview you must be able to edit appropriately. Someone new doesn't want to hear *all* about you. The idea is to tell people enough to keep it interesting, but keep it brief enough to avoid monopolizing the exchange. For example, if you meet someone new at a PTA meeting, you might say, "My name is Joan Walsh. I have children in third and fifth grade and help run the school book fair." This gives the other parent an opening to tell you about her children and perhaps express interest in volunteering.

9. Be Aware of Body Language

Body language is nonverbal communication that can aid or impede your efforts to meet and talk. At a cocktail party, people size you up in the first few seconds and decide whether they want to converse with you. Gestures, movements, facial expressions, and posture create an impression and can attract people to you or discourage them from approaching or building on a connection. What kind of impression do you make? Do you appear to be someone who is receptive to new people? If so, others are more likely to strike up a conversation with you. Does your body language convey confidence—or insecurity and fatigue? Eye contact is the most important body-language element when talking to people because it makes an instant connection. Add a smile and you look like you really want to be there.

As for posture, a relaxed, open stance welcomes people. Folding your arms in front of you or clasping your hands behind your back does not. And your mother was right: Stand up straight. If you tend to slouch, check yourself in front of a mirror and practice standing tall. When talking to people, avoid playing with your hair, tapping your foot, touching your face, or waving your hands around. You may want to punctuate what you're saying, but you're actually distracting the person.

And don't forget to keep your handshake firm to convey confidence and strength. If your palms tend to sweat, carry tissues in your pocket and blot. A consultant finds washing her hands with lots of soap and very hot water before attending an event keeps them dry for up to ninety minutes. In severe cases, you can also ask your doctor about a prescription product that dries sweaty palms.

10. Know How to Exit

At any social or business function, it helps to prepare your exit in advance. If you want to stay for only twenty minutes, don't sit down in a cushy armchair and nest. Keep the conversation brief and don't encourage people to tell you a long story, which will make it harder to extricate yourself.

If you'd really like to spend more time with someone, but you must move on to talk to another person, leave gracefully with "I want to talk more about this, but I have to attend the meeting," or "This information is really interesting. I want to hear more, but I must catch Amy before she leaves." On the other hand, if someone is really a clinger, you can lightly touch the person on the elbow and say, "Dave, it's been great speaking with you," turn obliquely (you don't want to turn your back), and walk away.

There's an art to judging when someone else wants to end a conversation with *you* and move on. The challenge is to learn to read signals. If the person you're talking to keeps glancing around the room or shifting from one foot to another, he/she isn't listening anymore. If you're getting one-word answers to your questions, the person may be bored. You can try switching to another topic, but if that doesn't work quickly, take the hint, go freshen your drink, and talk to someone else. You never want to overstay your welcome.

Be sensitive, too, to people who don't like questions about themselves. If someone changes the subject, you may have gone beyond the person's comfort limit. Tune in to such reactions and, to avoid becoming intrusive, adjust accordingly to a benign topic like sports or restaurants.

THE NAME GAME

Virtually everyone has trouble remembering people's names at social and business events, unless name tags are worn. When you're introduced to someone, as in "Joe, this is Pete Jones" or "Helen, meet my sister Suzy," say the person's name as soon as you hear it. Respond with "Pete, I'm glad to meet you." Or try "Ghada, where did your name come from [or what does it mean]?" Do the same after you walk up to someone and introduce yourself. Repeating names reinforces your memory of them.

Keep mentioning the person's name in conversation. Every time you do, you send the message "I know who you are.

You're important to me." Anyone responds well to that news, which is particularly vital in business situations.

It takes practice to sharpen your conversation skills, your awareness of other people, and your own reactions. If you feel embarrassed at the thought of trying out these rules of conversation, stand in front of the mirror and conduct a fictional conversation with someone before going to the meeting or the luncheon. Force yourself to hold your head up and look people in the eye. Eventually it will become easier. With time and patience, the rules can make a difference for you.

PART II

SOCIAL
OCCASIONS

3

PARTIES AND OTHER
SOCIAL EVENTS

Years ago, a friend invited me to a fundraiser for a philanthropy. The event included a cocktail party at a small, prestigious museum, plus a guided tour of the current exhibit. I knew none of the attendees, except for my friend, a board member who was busy attending to details and welcoming duties. On my own among wealthy guests, who tended to chat in tightly knit clusters, I wound up talking on and off to the hired photographer—and wondering why I hadn't sent a check and stayed home.

Perhaps you can identify with my experience. Although socializing is supposed to be pleasurable, it can feel like a minefield when you face a sea of strangers milling around with drinks in hand. You have to be prepared to initiate conversation, which may be difficult for you to do. If I knew then what I know now, I would have found ways to circulate more comfortably and, hopefully, enjoy the evening.

Cocktail parties can be fun if you know people. If you don't, you may dread standing alone trying to look confident. But you don't have to walk in "cold." You can call the person who invited you (or the sponsor organization) in advance, and explain, "I don't know anyone at the party. Who are some friendly people I can talk to when I walk in the door?" When you know others who you can seek out on arrival, you tend to feel calmer. You have something to do. Later, when you want to move on, you can look around for someone standing alone who seems congenial. Odds are the person will feel relieved to be approached and be happy to chat.

What do you say after you say hello? There are many possibilities when you tune in to the nature and purpose of the function.

BENEFITS FOR CHARITIES OR CAUSES

The arts, charities, and other worthy causes close to your heart (or important to a friend or business contact) deserve support. When you attend a benefit, you're expected to mix and mingle. A variety of conversation openers can smooth your way, beginning with "What is your connection to [name of institution or organization]?" If the person responds, "I'm on the board," you can continue with, "What projects are you involved in now?" or "What prompted you to get involved in the organization?" or "Tell me about volunteer opportunities." At the event I attended, I could have pointed to common ground with, "My friend is also on the board." A discussion of my friend's work for the charity might follow. At the same time, I would be giving credit to my friend and making her look valuable. Board members not only give money but also are expected to bring new people to the cause.

Conversation would take another path with someone not actively involved with the organization. For example, you might talk about the venue. At the event I attended, I could have discussed the museum and its ambience, as in, "What do you think of this setting [or the art tour]?" At a function held in a botanical garden, you might talk about the plantings or share tales of gardening challenges at home. Or you could inquire, "Have you attended other benefits for [name of organization]? How does this event compare?" Remember, open-ended questions stimulate continuing conversation.

One consolation at cocktail parties is they are time-limited. A stand-alone cocktail party usually lasts two hours, such as 6 p.m. to 8 p.m. Cocktails preceding dinner typically run an hour or so. In the latter case, you may be seated next to strangers at dinner. This is an opportunity to introduce yourself and ask tablemates, "What brings you here?" If someone sounds like an out-of-towner, pick up on it and inquire, "Where are you from?" That question almost always starts a dialogue. The last time I tried it, the answer was, "Originally from Minneapolis," which led to a discussion of regional accents and winters in Minnesota.

At a benefit for a nonprofit in the mental-health field, people at my table worked for a pharmaceutical company. To keep the conversation rolling, I asked them to elaborate with "Tell me about the drugs you market." I learned all about dosage issues and how they can affect a medication's sales.

ART GALLERY OPENINGS

Conversation topics are built in at gallery openings, where you can always talk about the show and its purpose, such as a summer roundup of local talent or a sculptor's latest work. To learn enough background to hold an intelligent conversation, go online and research the artist, gallery, and reviews of the work. The knowledge you gain will not only add to your appreciation of the show, it will give you more to talk about. You can ask the person standing beside you, "What do you think of the *Gazette*'s write-up? They loved the work." Or try, for example, "Did you know this is actually a photograph of thousands of tiny plastic soda bottles? You don't realize it when standing a few feet away." The person may reply, "Really? I'll have to look closer." And you're off to "Isn't it amazing," and so forth. Or ask, "Which sculpture do you like best?" and follow up with "Why?"

You might also mention a unique fact about the artist, as in "Who would guess the artist is eighty-five. Isn't it surprising how playful the paintings are?" This might lead to a discussion of artists who have produced great work in old age. At a van Gogh exhibit, someone opened a conversation with me by asking, "Did you know that van Gogh was a minister?" I did not, but the question led me to respond, "What is your interest in art?" which took our talk in another direction and led to a fascinating chat.

Other icebreakers might include "Are you an art collector?" If the answer is yes, follow with "What do you focus on?" When observing an inscrutable work, a great question is "What do you make of this?" If you're unfamiliar with the artist, try "This painter is new to me, but people say he's someone I should see. Can you tell me anything about him?" When you ask to be educated, you come across as curious, intelligent, and interested, rather than someone who is there only to see and be seen.

Incidentally, disagreement with the person you're talking to can be educational, too. If you ask someone, "How do you feel about Picasso?" the response might be "He's my favorite. I studied him in art classes at college." If you admit you're not a Picasso fan, your difference of opinion gives the person a chance to explain his or her view. The conversation can become more interesting.

Often you have a chance to meet the artist at an opening. This is a time for compliments, as in "You're so talented" or "I love your work" or "That painting over there speaks to my soul." If you dislike the work, keep it to yourself and focus instead on the creative process or how the artist's career got started. You might ask a photographer, "How do you choose your subjects?" or "What is your favorite photograph here, and why?" or "When did you first become interested in photography and what drew you to it?" As you learn more about the person, you learn more about the work and enrich your experience.

SCHOOL REUNIONS

High school and college reunions are occasions to ask yourself, "What do I hope to find here?" Maybe you're looking for old friends you haven't seen in years or wondering how classmates turned out. Some individuals are late bloomers. For others, high school may have been the pinnacle of their lives. Or perhaps you'd like to make new friends. A classmate you had little in common with years ago may be someone you'd like to know better today. Fellow alumni may also turn out to be important professional contacts.

A little preparation will help you get the most out of any reunion. Check out the school or alumni association Web site in advance for information on the program, as well as a list of alumni who plan to attend and other essentials. Then you can prioritize whom you most want to talk with. Contact the reunion committee especially if you're going alone. They may have helpful tips for you, including a list of people willing to share hotel accommodations.

The primary all-purpose question at any reunion is "What have you been doing all these years?" Ask it and be a good listener. After classmates have their say, it's your turn to update them about you. Maybe you weren't a cheerleader or football hero or academic achiever. This is your chance to be who you are today. Mention your own accomplishments, as long as you're not obnoxious about it. It's always best to let the facts speak for themselves. And beware of carrying emotional baggage from the old days. If you were shy in college but have become more outgoing since, act like it. You can break out of that old mold.

Reunions also offer a unique opportunity to reminisce about teachers, professors, and experiences, such as "Remember our jobs at McDonald's [or the time we almost flunked Spanish]?" Share memories of working on the school newspaper, the debating team, of sororities or fraternities. Photos from the old days are great connectors. If you have some, bring them along to pass around. Everyone will want to see them. Reunions are a place to get a glimpse of yourself as you were then. And of course there's always room for a bit of gossip about who else is (or isn't) there.

A downside of reunions is some people may be nonstop talkers or oblivious to boundaries and bring up painful experiences you'd rather forget. Just in case, keep an exit line handy. Simply say, "It's been swell talking to you. I just spotted my old roommate over there. See you later."

PERSONAL PARTIES

Many parties are more private and intimate than the events already mentioned. They may take place at someone's house or apartment (or occasionally at a restaurant) to celebrate a birthday or other occasion, or just to have fun. As a guest, it's important to participate and try to talk to everyone. Whatever the excuse for the party, you can always do the following:

- Ask, "How do you know the host and hostess?"
- Compliment, as in "Where did you get the great sneakers?"

or "What a beautiful watch." Or try "That's a great idea. How did you ever think of it?"

- Point out commonality, as in "You're in a barbershop quartet? So is my brother."
- Get curious. At one party I attended, a guest mentioned he was going to a license plate convention in Peoria. "Why are you interested in license plates?" I asked. He replied that he collected antiques and was fascinated by historical license plates and by laws governing plates in different countries. Among other things, I learned there is a limit on the number of cars a person can own in Singapore.

Guest of Honor Parties

Sometimes the party honors an out-of-town visitor. In such cases, you can pump the host or hostess for background information about the honoree beforehand. Then you can say to the visitor, "I'm so happy to meet you. I've heard so much about you." Such remarks make the person feel warmly welcomed and make you hard to resist. You can continue with something like, "How was your trip here?" or "I understand you just got back from Antarctica. Tell me all about it."

One woman got especially creative with a guest of honor, an Asian businessman who was her husband's client. She had been warned that the man spoke English but was very quiet. She walked over to him, introduced herself, and said, "How are you?" In a bored tone, he replied "Fine." Undaunted, she continued, "I have a little arthritis problem." And the man instantly came alive with interest. He replied, "I have arthritis, too. I cured myself with yoga." He proceeded to talk to her for forty minutes, demonstrating the exercises that worked for him and might help her.

"I had such a good time with him, which amazed my

husband," she recalls. "I find that men like to talk about jobs and health. Everyone forty-five or over either has arthritis or has a friend or relative who does."

This woman engaged the visitor by telling him a little more about herself than she usually would. It's a technique that works well at drawing people in and encouraging them to open up and share a bond.

Don't tell people more than they want to hear, of course. The conversation has to go back and forth. The person has to contribute something, and both of you must feel comfortable. If that doesn't happen, be ready to change the subject.

Housewarming Parties

The architecture of the new home and its furnishings are natural conversation openers, as in "What do you think of the new place, especially the backyard?" Or "Don't you wish you had a fireplace like this one?" Discuss the view or size of the rooms or the bathroom décor. If you're talking to the host or hostess, compliment the new place, of course, but you can also ask, "What is it like living in this area?"

At a get-acquainted-with-the-neighbors party, topics ranging from local taxes and the school system to garbage pickups are ideal. This is also the place to discuss local restaurants, shops, babysitters, and plumbers. Almost everyone has something to share that is interesting or useful.

Bridal Showers and Engagement Parties

You can ask other guests, "How long have you known Randy and Heather?" and adapt several of the conversation openers you'd use at weddings to bridal showers and engagement parties, as well (see pages 86–89). You can also ask the couple and/or parents, "How are the wedding plans progressing?" Ask the bride, "How is shopping for the wedding gown going?"

The highlight of a shower is opening gifts, and you can join in with enthusiastic comments, such as "What a great picture frame [or wedding planner]!"

Baby Showers

At one baby shower I attended, I didn't know many people. I walked in and said, "Hi, I'm a friend of Ken's mother. And you are?" I made a point of meeting the expectant mom's mother and grandmother and told them both what a lovely person Jean was. Baby names are another topic ripe for discussion. And of course it's easy to "ooo" and "ah" over all the adorable baby gifts as they are opened, as in "Isn't that the cutest blanket?"

At parties, people often ask, "What do you do?" When that happens, describe your occupation in a sound bite, and try to figure out an interesting way to do it. One man likes to say, "I'm a teacher-doctor," which inevitably leads people to ask, "What do you mean by that?" And he tells them, "I'm a professor with a doctorate in education. I train elementary school student teachers to be more reflective about their work and think about why they went into education in the first place." After speaking, the man reciprocates and draws in the other person with "How about you?"

You can also arm yourself with stories about your family to work into the conversation, such as "I've got two kids and they're twenty years apart." Always be prepared to switch over to the other person to bring him/her in.

OTHER SOCIAL ACTIVITIES

Often socializing is a byproduct of another activity entirely. For example, Meet the Candidates Night is fertile territory to meet people in your community. You already have something in common: you're neighbors and are interested enough in politics to show up. It's easy to start a conversation with "What do you think of [name of candidate]?" or "Who are you leaning toward and why?"

At a Dog Training Workshop you meet other pet lovers. All you have to do is admire the poodle over there and ask questions like, "What made you name her Letitia?" The conversation has begun.

When I took an advanced beginner class in bridge, I walked in and sat down with three strangers at a table. As introductions were made, I detected a foreign accent and asked the person, "What country are you from?" The answer was "Argentina," which triggered a conversation about personality differences between Argentineans and Brazilians. (The latter dance the samba as opposed to the tango.) When I mentioned my grandmother had lived in Argentina for several years, another player confided that some of his ancestors from Italy settled in Argentina. He wanted to locate them, which led to a discussion of genealogy. The point is, when you ask a question, you never know where it will take you.

You can share relevant news of your life that might interest the individual. A minute or two about boating in Chesapeake Bay or raising orchids might intrigue anyone. Just don't overdo it unless you've found a kindred soul.

Sometimes you see people you know, but not well. This is a time to remember information they mentioned the last time you met, as in, "How did you survive the IRS audit?" or "You said you were going to see your family in St. Louis. How did it go?" However, do not make assumptions and exclaim, "It must have been wonderful." Maybe it wasn't.

Recall issues you may have bonded over, such as a passion for volunteer work that helps children, and discuss them further. The person will feel flattered that you remain interested. Other questions or statements that encourage continuing conversation include these:

- "Tell me what's new and interesting in your life."
- "How's the family? What are the kids doing these days?"
- "What finally happened with . . . ?"
- "How are the singing classes [or the vacation plans] going?"

Ask yourself, "What do I really want to know about this person?" When I wanted to know more about someone from rural North Dakota, I said, "What's it like to live in a tiny town?"

The more you know and plan for social occasions, the better you're going to be at conversing and the more relaxed you're going to feel. As I was writing this book, I was invited to a large birthday party for a friend at a private club. I was told I might be seated with two well-known writers I had never met. That sounded interesting, but what would I say? After some thought, I decided to look up the books they'd written. Although I hadn't read them, I could mention them. I could also ask, "What are you working on now?" or "What's your next project?" Now there was plenty to talk about.

As you ask questions to clarify what's been said, common interests tend to reveal themselves, and you may just make a friend.

ROMANTIC VENUES
AND OCCASIONS

When you're open to (or looking for) romance, the issue is whether you can push past fears of rejection and find fresh ways to start a conversation or respond to an approach. The best strategies to show your interest avoid clichés and employ flexibility whether you're at a bar, party, club, or in another setting.

PAYING ATTENTION WORKS

Picture two guys in an outdoor café having dinner together. Topping one of their drinks is a little plastic sword, which proceeds to drop in the glass. Two women watching at the next table laugh out loud, as the man tries to fish out the sword. "We're sorry if we disturbed you," they apologize, still giggling. The men assure them they don't mind at all, and add, "Actually, we challenge you to a duel." Everybody roars, which sets the stage to continue talking. After dinner, the foursome heads for a bar and enjoys a great evening.

This story illustrates a first law of breaking the ice: be aware of what's going on around you, and use it to your advantage. When you do, what you say is spontaneous and original, rather than trite. Conversation flows naturally if you comment on what's happening in the moment, as the women in the café did. The men were able to pick up on their laughter and their apology as an invitation to continue the connection with a quip of their own. In a case where there is no "sword incident," you might use food as an excuse to open conversation in a restaurant, as in "What's that great-looking dish you ordered?"

At a bar, the catalyst could be as simple as noticing that someone attractive is nursing the same drink as yours. Since that's the common denominator, you might comment, "They make a good margarita here," or "Obviously we have the same taste in martinis."

Is someone appealing standing at the hors d'oeuvres table at a party? Maybe there's something unique about the person that you can comment on, such as a bandaged arm. That's an opening for "What happened to you?" If someone resembles a political figure or a movie star, you can strike up a conversation with, "You know, you look just like . . ." One couple met this way and dated for months. To extend chatting, ask an open-ended question, like "That's a nice tan. Have you vacationed someplace wonderful lately?"

"What do you do?" is stale and puts some people off. Yet vocation is important information in discovering what you have in common and sizing up someone. To coax it out differently, you might say, "My guess is you're an artist [or an engineer or a teacher]." The response "What makes you think that?" is guaranteed to follow, and you're into conversation. You can continue with "How did you get into it?" or "What do you like best about your work?"

When you're asked what *you* do, try a provocative response like "Tell me what you think I do."

Keep it light. Flirting is about being playful. Use humor if you're good at it, but try to relate it to what's going on. If you're a man and a sexy woman bumps into you at a party, you might quip, "I didn't know we were doing the rumba now. Would you care to dance?" It's natural to start talking after that opening. If you aren't a clever comic, at least try to lighten up wherever you are.

If you're feeling confident, self-deprecation is very attractive, too. When a guy asked about her cooking skills, an event planner retorted, "I don't cook. I warm." He laughed as she told him about prepared foods she bought and kept in the freezer.

GENDER-RELATED TIPS

Because men and women really are different, try the following strategies.

For Men

1. **Avoid boasting.** An office manager says, "One of the biggest mistakes guys make is talking about themselves to impress a girl. The biggest jerk at the party is usually the person who makes speeches about himself or brags about the money he made in real estate." Women respond to confidence, not arrogance, and gravitate toward someone who generates back-and-forth interchange. One way to draw in people is to seek advice, as in "I've been looking for an apartment rental downtown and can't find anything. Do you have any suggestions?"

2. **Show interest in her.** If you're used to talking about the weather, you may mention it right away. But it's usually

boring and the conversation isn't going to last very long. Instead try to demonstrate authentic interest in what she cares about and who she is. Ask, "So how do you spend your spare time?" or "What are your usual weekend plans?" If she's into crossword puzzles or the environment or is a vegetarian or wants to own her own company some day, these are safe topics to talk about. Comment on her views, ask open-ended questions, and listen attentively. Few men ask, "What are your interests; what are your dreams?" If you do, you're going to stand out. Look for points of commonality. Are you both Woody Allen or country-music fans?

3. **Compliment appropriately.** If you see an interesting woman holding an empty glass at a party, ask, "Hey, can I get that for you?" After you talk a bit and get good vibes, you can mention her pretty eyes or attractive earrings. Just don't open with that or she may consider it a "line."

4. **Read her body language.** Movements, facial expressions, and gestures are clues to whether a woman is receptive to you. Look for the signs. For example, if she plays with her hair, she's interested. If she smiles and makes eye contact, she's interested. However, if she starts looking around the room after a few minutes, she's telling you it's time to move on to someone else. Take the hint and don't be clingy.

   One man's motto is "Always leave them wanting a little more." After talking for a while, he excuses himself to go chat with a friend. "This shows her I'm social, and also gives her time to decide if she's interested in knowing me better," he says.

5. **Keep perspective.** Many men see a gorgeous woman and assume, "I have no chance with her," or "She must be dat-

ing. She's out of my league," when in fact she's sitting home on Saturday nights. Don't let discouraging self-talk stop you from approaching.

And remember, clever is nice if you're adept at it, but sincere works, too. You can never go wrong with a simple "Hi, I'm . . . ," accompanied by a smile on your face and "Can I buy you a drink?"

For Women

1. **Signal.** Women often think men have all the power, but even the hottest men can be terrified of rejection. It's easier for them to talk to you when you look as if you welcome attention. Get over fear of appearing too interested. It's up to you to signal your receptiveness and respond to overtures. Glance around, smile, and look like you're having a good time. Men won't come over if they think you don't want to be there. Don't cross your arms in front of you. That position communicates "Stay away from me." As you talk to a man, beware of looking away too often, or you'll give the impression you want to disconnect.

2. **Consider making a move first.** Men are usually the ones who initiate conversation, but many I've talked to find it very appealing when a woman approaches them. "I think it's the sexiest thing in the world if a woman walks up and offers to buy me a drink. Men like to be picked up as much as women do," says a banker. If he straightens his tie as you walk over, he's signaling he's interested.

Maybe you're standing on line with two friends waiting to get into a restaurant for Sunday brunch. Look around. Do you notice a cute guy alone? Why not ask if he'd like to join you and make it a full table? Who knows where it may lead?

Look for other ways to strike up a conversation. Are the men at the next table wearing jerseys for a sports team? You can say, "So you're [team] fans. How did the game go tonight?" or "Do you think [name of team] can win?" One gal noticed a patch on a guy's shirt, and asked "Are you a biker?" He was. "I went to Daytona just before Bike Week," she told him, and they talked the rest of the night. What if you're rebuffed? It happens. You aren't interested in everyone who approaches you, either.

Consider the case of a woman who went to a singles event at a university club where everyone was much younger than she. She spied a good-looking man with gray hair standing alone near the door who was about her age. He wore a navy blazer. Sashaying up to him bravely, a glass of white wine in her hand, she said, "You know, you're the only one here near my age and I thought I'd just say hello. I'm Sara." Smiling, he replied, "Hi, I'm with security."

3. **Position yourself.** Although you may not be accustomed to standing near the bar, it's a smart idea to position yourself there because that's where the traffic is. Maybe you see a guy you'd like to meet across the room. If you're near the bar when his buddy comes up to get drinks, you can ask, "What's your friend's name?" He'll go back and tell his friend, who will hopefully glance over and like what he sees.

When you're with friends, make yourself accessible. Stand at the edge of the group to make it easier for a guy to talk to you. He's unlikely to try if you're in the middle, surrounded by people, and he has to push through.

4. **Be polite.** Perhaps you're standing with friends and thinking, "I hope those guys near the door come over and buy us

drinks." Then someone else approaches you. You're not interested and give him a brusque brush-off. He walks away. Remember every man in the room can see what's going on—and chances are they won't like your behavior. Be kind when you turn down someone. If you turn off the rest of the room, no one else will approach you. Sometimes women are rude and then wonder why no one talks to them all night.

5. **Keep conversation positive.** Always keep in mind that men want to feel respected. To engage a guy, affirm what he tells you about himself, as in "That's really impressive," or "What a creative idea." Negative talk pushes people away. And remember, men like women with a sense of humor. Laugh at *their* jokes, too (if they're funny).

6. **Resist the cell phone.** Nothing turns off a guy faster than a phone in your ear. Switch it off. Many women say they have trouble meeting someone, yet they stand at a bar checking mail and text messages.

UNEXPECTED PLACES TO MEET

One woman meets men all the time at the supermarket. "Could you reach the chocolate?" she asks a six-footer at the ice cream freezer, and the conversation takes off. I met my husband on the elevator, asking the cliché question, "Don't I know you from somewhere?" (In this case I did.) Another couple met at a sale at Saks, and men and women meet all the time walking the dog. It's "Where did you get that adorable bull dog?" or "What's her name?" Other possibilities for meeting include the following places.

Trains and Planes

Maybe you're a sales manager on a commuter train and notice the cute blonde sitting next to you is writing in Chinese in a notebook. You turn to her and ask, "Are you an interpreter or an academic?" That's one way to strike up a conversation, and you may wind up talking nonstop. To extend the connection, as the train pulls into the station you might say, "Do you want to continue this conversation?"

Perhaps you're taking the train to the beach. The car is not crowded, and sitting across the aisle is someone attractive reading a book. If you're moved to talk, look over and ask, "What are you reading?" or "That seems to be an engrossing book." Or take another conversation path with "Do you know the closest stop to [name of town]?" Wait for the response, then briefly mention why you're going there, and continue, "Where are you headed?" Trains are comfortable venues for meeting because they're usually quiet and there's plenty of time for conversation.

Airplanes are well known for encouraging instant intimacy. One man noticed a gorgeous woman on line to board his shuttle flight. He decided to hang back and board after her, hoping the seat beside her would be available. It was, and he introduced himself. After she responded, he asked, "What takes you to Washington?" They dated for months afterward.

Of course you do have to take the hint when someone isn't responsive. A friendd of mine had just buckled in next to an attractive man in business class when the flight attendant appeared to check his ticket. There was a mix-up, and when the matter was eventually resolved, she turned to him and commented, "You must have been worried there for a while."

"No," he answered stiffly, burying his head in the newspaper. The only words he spoke the rest of the trip were, "Can I get past you?" as he headed for the restroom. Not everyone is friendly. Read your magazine.

On the other hand, another friend of mine met a great guy at O'Hare when their flight was canceled. You never know.

Museums

Is someone you think you'd like to meet standing in front of a sculpture that resembles a giant amoeba? Why not inquire, "What do you see?" or "Where would you put this in your home?" If the person is staring at an Andy Warhol silkscreen, you might try, "I have mixed emotions about pop art." Then wait for the response. The conversation can always move on to the subject of the museum itself or art auction prices—and perhaps continue over a cup of coffee at the café.

Health Clubs and Gyms

There are lots of props you can comment on or ask questions about in the gym, as in these examples:

- "Do you know where the towels are? I just joined."
- "How do you like it here?"
- "I'm looking for a personal trainer. Can you recommend one?"
- "Do you know where I can buy a combination lock?"
- "How do you rate the pool?"
- "What are the busiest times here?"
- "Where did you get that great gym bag?"

To encourage others to approach you, you might wear a T-shirt with an imprint that invites comment. While on vacation, a lawyer bought a T-shirt emblazoned with "Australia."

She loves to wear it to work out because men regularly ask her, "How did you like it?" or "When were you there? I've been thinking about going myself."

Bookstores

Comment on a book someone is carrying, as in "I've been wanting to read that. What do you think of his other novels?" Or mention the reviews, or ask, "What else have you read lately that you liked?" or "Can you recommend a really good political thriller?"

Questions and requests for advice are the easiest ways to start talking to someone, especially when you keep it light and related to where you are or what's going on around you.

MEETING ONLINE DATES IN PERSON

Curiosity, trepidation, and tension are built into an initial face-to-face encounter with someone you've met online. What if the person looks very different from the picture or comes across in a way that never surfaced online? If you like what you see, what can you talk about? There are ways to minimize disappointments or awkwardness.

Slow yourself down and consider whether you want to talk on the phone before agreeing to meet. It's all too easy to receive online replies, but phone conversation involves a whole new chemistry that provides more information. Perhaps the person's high-pitched laugh irritates you or he/she constantly interrupts you. If you're the impatient type, however, you may agree with a marketing manager who considers phone time a waste. "It's physical chemistry that's the ultimate make or break. A quirk on the phone may not bother you in person when you have the whole picture, and the best phone experience won't make a difference if you're not attracted to the person," he says.

When you do arrange to meet, plan ahead to avoid potential embarrassment and reduce anxiety. First, make it a brief encounter in a public place. Safety is an issue for women, and a short meeting gives you an escape hatch so you can leave fairly quickly if it isn't going to work. A drink at a hotel bar, coffee at a café, and lunch or dinner at a restaurant are all possibilities, as are museums of any kind. Museums lend themselves to conversation because you can always talk about the exhibit or the grounds.

Realize that you know something about the individual, but you don't know him/her well. Don't expect to improvise or chat extemporaneously on the spot. Instead, make a list of fun topics anyone likes to talk about, such as wine, movies, restaurants, or vacations. Keep them in mind for ready use in order to cut the risk of long, uncomfortable silences when you can't think of anything else to say. For additional conversation subjects, see pages 25–27. Don't feel you must talk about different topics with every new person. This is supposed to be fun, not work. Also think about questions you may be asked and prepare the answers.

If the meeting goes well, and you want to get to know the person better, be ready to pick up on background you've already learned. Pets and children, if the person has them, are "can't fail" topics.

You don't have to meet the person alone. You can include friends as a buffer to help yourself feel more comfortable. You might propose, "Hey, some friends and I are checking out this new wine bar. Do you want to join us?" Or "I'm seeing the new movie with friends. There's a great café nearby. Do you want to meet us there afterward?"

Your friends can stay a while, help stimulate conversation,

and then leave if the situation seems promising. Later they can give you an objective opinion of the person. If you're a woman, the presence of friends assures safety as well. Someone who wants to take advantage of you won't want to meet your friends, and will move on to someone else online.

People meet just about everywhere, and you can respond to the moment in any setting. A friend of mine vacationing in Paris once met members of the French Foreign Legion while having a drink with her sister at a bar. "I've always been fascinated by the Foreign Legion," she told the legionnaires. "What is your mission these days? Where have you been stationed?" She spent the evening enthralled by stories of their exploits. Someone else met his fiancée on a bus to Atlanta. When you're open, friendly, and interested, people tend to respond. Are you ready for possibilities, too?

5

DINNERS:
WHETHER HOST OR GUEST

What's the secret of a successful dinner party? It isn't the food or ambiance, although those ingredients are important. It's the people—and engaging conversation. The evening is a hit when guests enjoy talking to one another. If you're the host or hostess, it's up to you to help everyone connect. As a good guest, you're obligated to do your part and chat with others. Here's how to play either role constructively.

EFFECTIVE HOSTING

When I started entertaining many years ago, I tried to be the perfect hostess. I obsessed endlessly about the menu, spots on the silver, and over- or undercooking the roast. I spent the day of a dinner scrubbing and vacuuming the entire apartment. What if someone found a mite of dust under the bed? Since then I've learned a lot about orchestrating a memorable evening. What matters is helping people mingle and have a good time.

Making Guests the Priority

Your job as host or hostess actually begins with a welcome at the door. Because it's stressful to meet new people, guests often feel a bit tense and uncertain when they arrive unless they all know one another well. When you welcome them warmly and as if they are the only people in the world, you help them relax and let go. Start with an enthusiastic greeting, such as "I'm so glad you could come" or "It's great to see you. It's been too long." These statements instantly make guests feel wanted and send the message, "You're important to me. You're a VIP tonight."

Follow up by asking people what they'd like to drink—and help them get it. Or designate someone who arrived earlier to serve as bartender. Then you're free to devote yourself to the next guests at the door and put them at ease. This means you do not disappear for ten minutes to check the oven or tend to other chores and distractions. If necessary, delegate last-minute stovetop duties to someone else so you can focus your attention where it belongs: on your guests.

Facilitating Connections

All too often, dinner guests are introduced to one another quickly, then left to fend for themselves to initiate conversation. Because people are often shy, this may not work well. They may need you to take charge and help get a conversation going. You can provoke guests' interest in one another by following these steps:

- **Provide background.** Don't stop at "Mary, this is Pete." Add "Pete just changed jobs and moved here from Santa Fe." This gives Mary enough information to ask how Pete likes his new company and is adjusting to the new area. Or try, "Pete just bought one of those new condos downtown," which might lead to a discussion of local development.

- **Explain guests' relationship to you.** It might be "Roz and I worked together at IBM after college [or went to summer camp together as kids]." A discussion of the pros and cons of camp (or IBM) might follow. Or perhaps you and Roz are tennis partners, which could lead to talking about tennis clubs or the matches on TV.

- **Mention what they have in common.** Introduce one guest to another in the same business, as in "Bob is also a financial planner" or "Tom works in the same health care field you do." Or try "Helen, I want you to know Martha just had a baby, too, and also works at home a few days a week." As they compare notes on career and child care issues, you can excuse yourself and move on to other guests.

Other options might include "You've both volunteered for political campaigns. You're going to have a lot to say to each other." Or "Mark is a Dolphins fan, too." Or "Weren't you thinking of a trip to Prague? Angela just got back."

If people don't know each other, it's impossible to predict for sure how they'll hit it off. In cases where guests are already acquainted, the challenge is supplying information that triggers further exchanges, as in "Harold, did you know Steve is buying a Porsche?" Then Harold might reply, "I always wanted a Porsche. What model did you get?" Or try "Jim had the same problem with his birch trees that you do."

Choosing Guests

To some extent you can control opportunities for conversation through the guest list. Interaction isn't an issue when people are old or close friends. They're accustomed to hanging out together. But you may want to add fresh faces to the mix. To get people talking, mention something unusual or provocative about the new person, as in "Hank just sold his house and bought a farm." Everyone will want to know why he did it and what farm life is really like.

Ideally, include a guest who can talk about interesting experiences or passions. I was at a dinner where the host introduced someone this way: "Joe just got back from the Cannes Film Festival." Naturally we all pumped Joe about the best entries and the juiciest movie star gossip. Another good choice is someone from another country who can supply another slant on international events in the headlines.

If possible, invite someone with a good sense of humor who will keep everyone laughing and/or an intellectually curious person who will help draw out other guests so you don't have to do all the work. Someone good at talking to anyone can jump-start a conversation, then walk away after a few minutes to engage the next person.

Seating Arrangements

Plan seating with points of similarity in mind. Two shy or quiet people seated next to each other probably won't work, but the combination of someone who just bought a country house and a landscape designer might. Seat a great golfer next to someone else who loves the sport. Be sure to point out to them what they have in common. One hostess makes notes about why she might seat two people together. Maybe both attended the University of North Carolina—or both have daughters at Duke. She jots down "Daughters/Duke" to remember it. Then she can say, "You'll enjoy sitting next to Debbie because her daughter is a year younger than yours and also at . . ."

Although you want people to be compatible, differences can stir fascinating discussions. People of opposing political persuasions can be stimulating as long as they're willing to listen to other points of view and understand the boundaries of friendly disagreement. If you sense tempers rising, however, you may have to intercede and change the subject.

Separating couples and seating them apart can also change the dynamics at a dinner. However, some people may refuse to cooperate. They may feel insecure on their own or depend on the partner to serve as a buffer. As one husband explained, "When my spouse does most of the talking, I can sit back, relax, and just listen."

Launching Discussion

Once people are seated, they may continue conversations begun over drinks. When that doesn't happen, you can act as moderator. At one dinner I attended, the hostess asked an oncologist, "What's the biggest development in cancer treatment these days?" Naturally everyone at the table was riveted by the response. At another dinner, one guest asked the young mother of a three-year-old, "Jill, tell us what you're doing for yourself lately." Jill proceeded to explain how she turned a vague idea for a home-based picture-framing business into a thriving enterprise.

It helps to make a list of topics in advance to encourage people to talk—the more unusual, the better. A statement like "Jerry, tell us about your night in jail in Belgium" will get people's attention. So will a couple that celebrated their twentieth anniversary at an ice hotel in Canada. Feel free to add your own experience. Catastrophes can be hilarious, such as the Thanksgiving you dropped the turkey on the floor or the time the caterer disappeared and you had to order in pizza.

Creative Devices

There are also unexpected ways to involve guests with one another. One option is to write a comic quip about the person on each place card. Individualized fortune cookies would achieve a similar effect, generating laughter as people go around the table reading theirs out loud. A friend of mine once hired a palm reader for her dinner party. Guests got to know one another as they listened and traded comments.

For a themed occasion, a hostess may throw a square-dance dinner party where guests arrive to find a fiddler and a caller. Another idea to warm even the coldest, rainiest night: hire an accordionist to play for an hour as people walk in the door. Why? Because it's kitschy and makes you laugh out loud. When was the last time you heard an accordionist playing "Roll Out the Barrel" and tapped your foot? Anything unlikely kick-starts conversation (and the entire evening).

Games can also involve and connect guests who love challenges—and encourage people who aren't verbally expressive to join the fun. For example, at a dinner with a sports theme you might propose, "Let's play a game where everyone comes up with a sports factoid." A normally quiet, reserved athlete would probably shine.

Or you can keep it very simple and still get conversation rolling with "Let's go around the table. Describe the last great fun thing you did."

Winding Down

Toward the end of the evening, I often lead guests from the dining area to the living room for coffee and/or after-dinner drinks. Just getting up and walking over to a new setting recharges everyone and allows them to talk to people who were seated at the other end of the table.

This move is also a nice preliminary to saying good night. Both the first ninety seconds of a dinner party and the last set the stage for guests to feel connected. To reinforce warm feelings, always accompany people to the door. As they leave, tell them how much you've enjoyed their company.

If you're at ease, circulating, and having a good time, your guests probably are, too. On the other hand, they are aware of your absence if you're constantly in the kitchen being a drudge. It's important to be available to your guests. Can you really handle a sit-down dinner for fourteen? Few of us can without help. Order in if that's more comfortable and you can afford it, or cater or hire a cook or someone to wash dishes. Know your limits. Consider whether you'd prefer one big dinner or two small, intimate dinners. If a dinner feels too intimidating, think about lunch or brunch, which are simpler and less formal.

BEING A GOOD GUEST

Conversation can make or break a dinner party, which is why a good guest does more than just show up; he or she makes an effort to participate and chat with people. You will also endear yourself to the host or hostess if you act as a connector and introduce those you've met to others.

An obvious icebreaker is "How do you know [name of host or hostess]?" You can also eavesdrop on conversations around you for tidbits to use to initiate a chat. You may learn that the guy in the gray suit just received a promotion or the couple on the couch recently married. When you get a chance, you can open a conversation with, "Congratulations. Where did you go on the honeymoon?"

Talk to Everyone

As a guest, it's in your best interests to be inquisitive and learn about other guests. Once seated, be sure to speak with the person on your left as well as the one on your right. On the other hand, don't monopolize one person at the dinner table, and do be sensitive to the host's responsibilities. It's rude to expect to have a long private conversation with him or her. This is not the time for a heart-to-heart about your ex.

Keep up with current events and read the newspaper or listen to TV news for conversation starter ideas. Once you start thinking about possible conversation paths, it's surprisingly easy to find them. For example, I'm not an authority on classical music, but I am curious. I might ask a pianist or a symphony conductor about favorite concert halls and why they're preferred. If you were seated next to a basketball coach and knew nothing about the sport, you could ask, "What is the biggest challenge in coaching a team?"

You never know when you'll make a valuable contact. When I was starting out as a writer, it was at a dinner party that I met an editor who wound up giving me my first article assignment for *Reader's Digest*.

When talking to someone you've met before, try to remember and use information from a previous conversation you had, as in "How did your house hunting turn out?" Or "You once told me you belong to the Jane Austen Society. Are you still involved in that?" When conversation lagged at one dinner, I remembered that someone at the table was a big fan of jazz. "Tell us about the music scene these days," I said. He proceeded to bring us up to date on jazz in our area and regaled us with anecdotes. Other guests commented and asked questions. It was a stimulating evening.

Say Thank You

Leave graciously at the end of the evening, and thank your host or hostess with some enthusiasm, as in "I had such a good time. I'm sorry the evening is over," or "What a wonderful evening. Thank you for including me." Follow up with a handwritten thank-you note, with words such as "Your dinners are always so special, and last night's was one of your best. I especially enjoyed talking to Roger, whom I'd never met before. Thank you for a memorable evening. Love, . . ."

I've been to gorgeous dinner parties that were deadly dull and backyard barbecues I didn't want to leave. What made the difference was lively conversation and interaction. As a host or hostess, it takes effort and concentration to get people talking together. But when you light the match of conversation, you provide the setup for a good time.

If you're a guest, mingle, listen well, have good manners, and make eye contact. The host or hostess will appreciate your help in creating a successful evening and ask you back. Certain people are always in demand as dinner guests. Wouldn't you like to be one of them?

FAMILY GATHERINGS

Visits to relatives and friends are the most popular form of leisure travel—for understandable reasons. Caring families are a refuge. We're drawn to bond with one another and we want our children to know the security of grandparents, aunts, uncles, and cousins. But the ties that bind are complicated today. Your family may be scattered in other states or other countries. Even if logistics aren't a problem, there may be issues of blended families to contend with. Yet no matter how often you see one another—and regardless of tensions that may exist—you can carry basic conversation strategies with you to maximize the pleasure of holidays, reunions, and other family get-togethers.

THE ROLE OF FAMILY SCRIPTS

If tensions tend to arise when your family gathers periodically, you can probably write the script of who will say what, who will get upset, and who will needle who. You may feel helpless to change the scenario, yet you can prepare for hot-button issues and do something different to break out of negative patterns. Maybe your aunt always asks you about your daughter's poor school performance. You know that's going to lead to criticism of your parenting practices. The implication is that your child would be a model student if only she was raised right.

Or perhaps your brother-in-law regularly asks whether your business is doing okay—and you know you're going to hear his critique of your management style. You may feel tempted to make a direct statement like "I really don't want to talk about this because we're just going to get into a fight." But that usually fans the flames. In contrast, humor is a great diversion. The next time your aunt makes an irritating comment, say something funny like "Sometimes I think I'll send my daughter to the moon." This kind of transition makes everyone laugh and defuses the tension. Follow that with a change of subject, such as "Hey, did you hear about the news yesterday that . . ."

Karen Gail Lewis, a family therapist in Cincinnati and Washington, D.C., observes that ordinarily you get angry, defensive, and feel hurt when someone criticizes you. "You respond as you always do, and that encourages others to respond as they always do. But you can change that scenario when you prepare. Know your script and walk around it as soon as you feel set up for a bad scene," she says.

If humor isn't your strong suit, enlist friends to suggest funny comebacks you can keep on tap. Practice the lines until they seem natural to you. It helps to tell yourself, "I don't have to be nervous. I'm going to prepare for this the way I prepare for a job interview or anything important."

Sometimes the script involves family members who are not good friends and always talk unpleasantly about each other— or who are simply boring. Here you can use another strategy to change the script: give people something to do. Arrive with a game that requires them to interact, something uncomplicated that will appeal to the whole group. If some people aren't great with words, avoid Scrabble. On the other hand, pick games that involve working as teams, such as Charades. Board and card games work because the family laughs and plays together. Choose fun games that are short. Keep them light. Avoid games that become so competitive that they cause family conflict. An option is to bring several games or visit a game store and ask for advice.

Other changes help, too. If large gatherings seem to cause someone to act out, try getting together in smaller groups. Consider different locations, perhaps taking turns hosting holiday dinners. We all have different entertaining styles, which can lead to new experiences for everyone. If Thanksgiving dinner is served at your house, instead of at your mother or mother-in-law's home, roles change. Invite in a few friends or distant relatives to add to the mix, and you change the dynamic. Or consider going to a restaurant, rather than someone's home, to shake up the routine (and eliminate cleanup chores in the process). A new setting can make an enormous difference.

DO YOUR PART

Recognize sensitive topics in your family and stay away from them. If a couple is having infertility problems, chances are they don't want to be asked, "Anything new yet?" That's why "Tell me about your life" is such a useful statement. You can pause and wait for them to mention the subject on their terms if they wish. It's one thing to ask someone who was laid off "How are you?" It's another to inquire "Have you gone on any interviews lately?" which can make the person feel pressured or harassed.

Never criticize someone's spouse or child. Parents can complain about their youngsters. *You* cannot unless you want to risk resentment. Do not speak ill of the dead, either. They get special dispensation. And steer clear of controversy. I remember two occasions in my childhood when my father and uncle almost had fistfights over candidates for president. Do not try to persuade someone of your position, no matter how deeply held your beliefs. It won't work.

If you and your sister or brother consistently squabble at get-togethers, maybe it's best to circulate with other family members on these occasions. Old issues between siblings, such as jealousy, are more likely to be activated when parents are present.

Sometimes other people's arguments arise out of seemingly innocent conversations and a referee is needed. At a birthday party, for instance, your mother and aunt start fighting over which one looks most like your grandmother. It goes downhill from there and they rally their own teams. It may be necessary for a third party to separate them, and the sooner it's done, the better. Such "silly" fights can cause major (and lasting) rifts. Step in early. Touch your aunt's arm, steer her away, and ask for her brownie recipe.

Sharing milestones nourishes us, but occasions like a child's graduation can be touchy if you have a stepfamily and your spouse's ex is "difficult." One stepmom made a point of saying, "This is such a special day. Everyone should be proud of Jason." The words were water on a flickering flame. At other times she glides through the situation by asking herself, "What would Jacqueline Kennedy do? How would someone I admire handle this?"

Another woman, who has adult stepchildren who can be trying, looks at family occasions this way: "It's only one day, and we can suck it up for the grandkids."

WHEN YOU SEE ONE ANOTHER FREQUENTLY

If your family is fortunate enough to get together regularly, these are probably pleasant occasions where comfortable conversation flows naturally. But shifts from the same old, same old can be stimulating and fun. Why not make a list of brand-new topics that the family has never talked about before? Questions like these encourage everyone to imagine and think in areas that are safe and nonthreatening:

- "If we were all to move, where would we want to go?"
- "If you could have your choice of any job you wanted, what would it be?"
- "If you changed your first name, what would you choose and why?"

Or take turns going around the table answering the question "What was the high point of your week [or month or year]?" As each person answers, others comment and meaningful discussion is underway. At Thanksgiving, a question might be "What are you most thankful for this year?"

Another way to warm up everyone is to pull out the family photograph albums. Then you can sit on the sofa squealing together as you look at baby pictures or wedding and vacation photos. Changing patterns involving the children can add interest and fun, too. If you always send them to another room to play, why not have them stay? If the kids are always present, maybe it's time to let them go off separately. The point is almost any shift shakes up interactions and admits fresh air.

INFREQUENT VISITS

It may be harder for everyone to reconnect when family visits are few and far between. Although the Internet makes it relatively easy to stay in touch, and there is always the phone, not everyone uses these modes of communication regularly, and they cannot replace the intimacy of face-to-face contact. You can't hug someone on your cell.

Once you're in the same room, you may feel awkward together at first. You may not know very much about the details of one another's daily lives, and it may take time to slip back into comfortable, familiar relationships. You can move along the process by setting a warm tone from the start. Greet everyone with a smile on your face as soon as you arrive.

It's common to try to reconnect with questions such as "What's going on with the kids?" or "How is business?" But a more meaningful way to become reacquainted is to say, "Tell me about your world. How are you doing?" These are words that demonstrate sincere interest and encourage thoughtful conversation.

Another way to renew ties is to reminisce about shared experiences. You can bring up happy family memories with "Do you remember when . . . ?" In my family, memories of excursions to Brighton Beach with cousins and card games in the sand get us laughing out loud. Consider in advance which experiences are likely to get the best reception and have them in mind, ready to pull out when the time is right. Glance through your family photo album for ideas. Recalling good times is always a way to rediscover deep connections and leaves people wondering, "Why don't we do this more often?"

You can also talk positively about family members who are missing. Bonding takes place when you all share caring feelings or genuine worry about someone who didn't attend the occasion. Trashing someone has the opposite effect. It sets a bad precedent and brings the whole family down.

TALKING TO CHILDREN

Many adults feel awkward conversing with young relatives. It's different from communicating with their own kids. If this describes you, you may find it difficult to get to know nieces, nephews, and other youngsters you see infrequently. The common fallback question is "How's school?" because you don't know what else to say. The child usually answers "Okay," and that's the end of the chat. To elicit a meaningful response and get a real conversation going, try these questions instead:

- "Who's your best friend? What do you like most about her/him? What do you do together?"
- "Do you like to read?" If the answer is yes, continue with "Tell me about your favorite books [or about the last book you read]." If the response is, "I like the Little House books," you can mention that you or your children also liked them.
- "What are you doing after school?" A ten-year-old is likely to have a gazillion things going on.
- "I like the shirt [or jeans] you're wearing. Did you pick it out yourself? Why do you like it so much?"
- "What do you do on Saturdays?" This works especially well for a youngster who isn't an avid reader. Some children are very shy and won't open up, but others will tell you they play soccer and like the uniform.

The idea is to focus on the child and find something he or she wants to talk about. For example, if a six-year-old has lost a few teeth, you might say, "Looks like you've had a visit from the tooth fairy." Pause for the response, which might involve the going rate for a missing tooth these days and lead you to talk about how much you or your children got for a tooth years ago.

Teens

Teenagers have a small world that revolves around friends and school. Many of them feel stuck at a family function and would rather be anywhere else. Although kids may not feel comfortable with adults, they do want to talk to them. They just don't know how. To draw them out, ask specific questions, as in "What are your summer plans?" or "What sports are you into?" If you know a teen is into martial arts or magic, ask or comment on the activity, as in "Can you show me your latest trick?" Older teens may be passionate about social issues like global warming or alternative energy. You can ask for their thoughts and listen to and value their feelings, even if they may seem a bit naïve to you.

Avoid making assumptions about whether a child is going to college. For example, a youngster who wants to be a chef may feel working in a restaurant is better experience. You don't want to put the teen on the spot. If teens don't feel pressured, they'll talk. On the other hand, if you know a high school student is interested in music as a career, you might ask "So what's your dream career in the music field?"

If a teenager (or a younger preteen) is difficult to talk to, you can always ask for help programming your cell phone or fixing a glitch on your computer. It's a way in, and there aren't many things kids can do that adults can't. Everyone likes to be asked to do a favor.

If you really want to know a child, issue an invitation to come visit with you for an overnight—or, if you live nearby, to see a new comedian or a show coming to town or a ball game. The role of aunts and uncles is underappreciated and tremendously valuable to kids.

CONVERSATIONS WITH THE ELDERLY

Some people, due to discomfort about disabilities or other issues, feel awkward and uncertain when talking to the elderly. Yet it's respectful to make an effort to speak with older family members, and everyone benefits from their knowledge of family history and folklore. That enriches us all—and can be passed on to younger generations.

It's easy to find something meaningful to say when you know how. Try these approaches, which can be especially helpful when you're visiting at an assisted living facility or nursing home:

- Encourage older relatives to share stories of their lives. Ask Great-uncle Moe "What was it like to be drafted?" Stories can help you figure out family mysteries or secrets that always baffled you, such as why Aunt Rebecca never married or why Uncle Jim was the family favorite.
- Ask for advice, as in "What did you do when your kids wouldn't sleep [or had tantrums]?" You can learn from older relatives' experience and wisdom, and they feel useful.
- If the person has been ill or has a chronic health problem like diabetes, ask, "How are you managing?"—and listen.
- Compliment. Try "Grandma, you look so pretty in that dress, all the men must be chasing you" or "Grandpa, I

don't know what I'd do without you to fix things around here." Such comments are a boost to their self-esteem.

- Ask about their lives now, as in "Tell me about your favorite activities these days." You may be surprised. Great-uncle Al may work out at the senior center. Great-aunt Marian may win bridge tournaments.
- Remember to give a hug, a kiss, or a touch on the shoulder now and then. If someone has hearing loss, speak clearly and loudly enough. If you ask a savvy child to introduce an older relative to the computer, you'll be doing both of them a favor.

Families are imperfect—even the ones that may seem ideal to casual observers. But in this stressful, uncertain world, it helps to know we have each other. To reach for the good times, relax, hang on to your sense of humor, and focus on the bonds you share. Using the conversation tools you've learned, you can increase the pleasures of connection.

7

VACATIONS AND TRAVEL

Several years ago, my husband and I had dinner at Brasserie Flo in Paris (no, I couldn't resist my namesake). We were the only Americans in the place, and we listened as a couple at the next table proceeded to order mixed seafood. When the enormous platter arrived, I said to the pair in halting high school French, "Formidable! Why didn't we order that?"

All of us laughed and started talking. Although they spoke fractured English and our French was limited, that was part of the fun. We learned that he was a physician in Rouen and she worked for a pharmaceutical company. They and their children were visiting his family, and the grandparents were babysitting. We gabbed the whole night about everything from French medicine to American movies.

The evening was a highlight of our trip, which is why the question "Who can I meet and what can I learn?" has special meaning when you travel. New people surround you wherever you go, and you're apt to be more open and relaxed away from home. The anonymity factor helps in this regard. Nobody knows who you are, and you can say anything you want without worrying "What will they think?" You're probably never going to see them again.

Conversation openers like "Where are you from?" work on a trip to the Grand Canyon as well as abroad. Other options include "What brings you here?" or "Where else have you been?" In addition, particular activities actually encourage conversation. Stay aware of them and you can enhance your good time.

MEETING WHEN EATING

As my experience illustrates, restaurants often present opportunities to chat with people. Wherever you are, when you're in the mood to reach out, all you have to do is turn to someone at the next table and try one of these icebreakers:

- "May I ask what your dish is? It looks wonderful."
- "The waiter isn't very friendly, is he?"
- "Do you know the specialties of the house?"
- "What do you think of this place?"
- "Do you know what the guidebooks say about this restaurant?"

Restaurants are also places to pick up on what you overhear. In an upscale restaurant famous for its chef, I once sat next to an Irish couple with teenage children. The sixteen-year-old requested the equivalent of Chicken McNuggets and French fries. When I made eye contact with the mortified parents, we shook our heads and burst out laughing. Then we discussed teenage tastes and moved on to family life in Dublin.

It's true that some people aren't receptive to chatting, and it's important to respect their privacy. Many others are happy to talk to you.

STANDING ON LINE

When you're cued up for admission to cultural attractions or on tours, you can easily and naturally talk to people next to you about the scenery, the architecture, the history you're about to see, or the local food. As you wait to buy theater tickets, you can discuss reviews, the cast, other shows, and even ticket prices. It passes the time and you can learn valuable information, such as how to get discounts or where to go for after-theater dining.

There's companionship in adversity on airport lines. If you're stuck inching through customs in Mexico with hundreds of other weary passengers, it helps to share the misery and discuss frustrations with someone behind you. You can try conversation openers like these:

- "Where did you get your luggage? It's just what I'm looking for."
- "How clever to tie a red ribbon on the baggage handle! You can spot it immediately on the carousel."
- "Are you familiar with our hotel?"
- "Where do you like to eat here?"
- "Can you recommend interesting side trips?"

I met an Australian schoolteacher while standing on line with friends at a London museum café. She asked the waitress for a table for one. The response was, "There's a wait." Overhearing the exchange, we invited her to join us at our table. What a fascinating lunch. We learned all about her home city, Perth, and her experiences teaching Aborigine children.

Or you can launch the conversation by asking the people on line ahead of you "Have you been waiting long?" or "What did you think of the exhibit?" Be brave and take a chance.

When you're alone, after chatting a while, you might even ask, "Can I join you?"

STAYING AT HOTELS AND RESORTS

Asking to be included is a life skill worth practicing on vacation. If you wear a smile on your face and seem friendly, the answer is likely to be yes much of the time. Maybe you and your spouse or partner are spending a week in the Caribbean. You notice some people playing volleyball and walk over to ask "Can we play, too?" The answer will likely be "Sure." After you get home, you may even socialize with some players who live nearby. This is one way for couples to expand their social circle.

Many resorts sponsor contests or other activities that encourage guests to interact with one another. Hotels understand that connecting with other vacationers is part of the fun. The more socializing going on, the greater the chances you'll have a great time and come back.

The pool is another place to meet people. Maybe you're a woman who comments to another guest on the next chaise longue, "Oh, that's such a cute bathing suit you're wearing." As you start chatting yourselves, one of your mates loosens up and says to the other, "Hey, can I get you a beer?" Soon they're talking, too. An interesting or unusual occupation also gets conversation going. For instance, if one person is a cop, everyone wants to know about that.

You never know where casual chats may lead. Someone on the beach in Maui started talking to another sunbather about iPods. Eventually they progressed to the subject of work and discovered they were both college professors who ran consulting businesses. They exchanged business cards, e-mailed after they got home, and may work together on a project. Some-times personal and business networking intertwines to every-one's benefit.

CRUISE VACATIONS

Cruises are special cases because opportunities to socialize are built in. You're part of a contained community for a set num-ber of days and nights. You meet people wherever you go, and it's natural to chat while engaging in the various activities. Enter the elevator and somebody says, "These elevators are difficult to figure out, aren't they?" which leads you to ask, if there's time, "How are you enjoying the trip?" If you see the person in the halls or at lunch, you're now acquaintances. It feels comforting when you know people.

Before or after the Pilates or bridge class, you might ask, "What do you think of the instructor?" Or start talking to the person in the next deck chair. It's friendly to comment on the ship, the shops, the ocean or to inquire, "How do you like your cabin?"

You're usually asked to dine with other guests on a cruise unless you've requested a separate table. Everyone's concerned about getting stuck with boring people, but you always have a way out. The headwaiter can usually switch your table on request. But take a chance and you may be pleasantly sur-prised. On a *Queen Mary* transatlantic crossing with my fam-ily, we were seated next to an English family. The mix of age groups stimulated lively conversation at dinner together every night.

When my family was otherwise occupied, I was often alone for breakfast or lunch. In the dining room, I was asked to join passengers I didn't know. I always said yes. Usually I was ush-ered to a table where everyone sat in silence, uncertain what to say. I consciously decided to practice the role of hostess to get people talking. I said, "Hello. My name is Florence. I'm from New York. How about you?" The couple to my right was South African. On my left were two women from the suburbs of Toronto. Other people were Austrian. As we went around the table, everyone started loosening up. Some people compared the ship to others they had cruised on. One pair announced they were taking the *Queen Mary* round trip—a twelve-day vacation. We went on to discuss the employment picture in Canada and education in Pretoria, South Africa. By the end of the meal, we were comfortable friends.

It's easier than you think to orchestrate conversation in this way, even if you've never done it before. Just consider it a public service—for yourself as well as everyone else—and keep in mind possible questions you want to ask. People tend to be relieved and grateful when someone else leads the way. They almost always want to talk. They just don't know how to start.

OTHER RECREATION

There are many kinds of vacations, of course. One couple spent eight days and nights with a group of strangers on a rafting trip down the Colorado River. They used a favorite device to get to know people: asking couples how they met. A husband and wife from San Francisco met in a Dumpster. Each had moved into a new apartment and was scavenging for furnishings. Such stories lead others to relate their own experiences and everyone gets to know one another. If a pair met while walking a picket line, who doesn't want to hear the details?

Other people enjoy diving vacations. A great way to learn more about the sport is to strike up conversations with fellow enthusiasts, as in "How long [or where else] have you been diving?" or "What are your favorite dive spots?" or "Are your spouse and kids with you?"

Perhaps you and your partner are at a tennis camp, standing around waiting for the clinic to start. You overhear that other guests are South American. You approach them and say, "We hear you're from Peru. We went there last year." The response is likely to be, "Where did you go?" If you're compatible, you may hang around together for the next few days.

If you notice what's going on and pick up on it, even a sale at the golf and tennis shop encourages conversation. One woman turned to another customer to inquire, "Do you play tennis?" The response was, "I used to, but my husband got too good for me. Now I play golf." Later on they met again, and the first woman greeted the husband with "I hear you're a good tennis player." The stage was set to socialize.

TRAVELING ALONE

Solo vacations can be lonely unless you make an effort to reach out, as a colleague of mine did when she spent four days at a spa. She talked to people in her exercise classes and joined a communal table for meals. When alone at the snack bar, she noticed someone at the next table reading a book as she chewed on a sandwich. She asked, "Can you get snacks in the afternoon in the dining room?" and "What are your favorite classes?" Later she followed with "What do you think of the nutritionist?" and "Which lectures have you attended?" When you talk about something relevant, conversation moves along. In the process, people reveal little bits of information about themselves that can lead to further exchanges.

Of course you must be prepared for rejection in any social interaction. On the morning hike, this woman suggested to another guest who seemed congenial that they join up later for lunch. The person made it clear she was with a friend and wanted no other company at meals. The response stung but passed quickly. Some people have agendas that don't include you. Forget it and move on.

You can plan ahead to make traveling alone easier. Use bits of information gleaned from travel guides, such as inexpensive places to shop, to start conversations on tours. Pick cruises and tours that cater to your interests and attract at least some people in your age group. One woman on a cruise was asked to start a table for dinner. She was happy to oblige because it gave her something to do. She assembled a congenial mix of a dentist from Scotland, two American couples, and herself for an evening of stimulating conversation.

There are so many singles today that the travel industry is sensitive to this market. Group tours and clubs can match you with other solos to share trips and accommodations. There are even singles clubs for RV travelers.

"Traveling is the best time to talk to strangers. It's an opportunity to try out your new material—like a comedian on the road. If it doesn't fly, no harm done," says a public relations executive.

Some couples choose to vacation by themselves, rather than with friends, because they know they'll be more likely to talk to new people that way. "It's part of our adventure," says a wife. "We see our friends all the time at home."

I try to talk to locals wherever I am, and find that people appreciate it when you attempt to speak their language, regardless of your fluency. It's a good way to meet, have fun, and get help and advice when you need it.

(8

WEDDINGS

Relatives or friends of the bride and groom probably know many of the guests and feel comfortable circulating at a wedding. But often you're connected only to the parents or you have business ties to the couple that might leave you feeling adrift in a sea of strangers. You are still expected to talk to people and honor this very important day. If you're the bride and groom, you're the center of attraction and have a different role to play. In either case, here's how to mix and mingle successfully.

GUESTS

If you're rolling your eyes at the thought of chatting with a crowd of distant acquaintances or people you've never met, recognize that you can take steps to feel more comfortable and have a good time. First, arrive early at the wedding to avoid the stress of rushing and jockeying in the parking lot to secure a convenient spot. Punctuality also gets you a good seat at the ceremony—plus a chance to talk to people you might know at least slightly (and introduce yourself to those you don't). These are guests you can chat with again later at the reception.

At one memorable wedding I attended alone, the only people I knew well were the parents of the groom—and they were very busy. I tried my best to strike up conversations with other guests throughout the evening. Since we were all connected in some way to the bride, groom, or their families, I focused on that commonality. I introduced myself with the basics: "Hello, I'm Florence. And you are?" I followed with, "I'm a neighbor of the groom's parents. How do *you* know [names of the couple]?" Another option is, "Which side of the family are you on?" If both of you are linked to the bride's family, you can chat about people you know in common. If not, you might educate each other about your respective sides. Or try "How did you meet John or Laura?" The responses can be surprising. In one case, a guest met the bride on jury duty, and she proceeded to tell the story of the unusual trial.

For many people, a wedding also lends itself to conversations about fashion. You can open with "I love your dress [or shoes or clutch bag]." After the response, you can move on to "Where did you get it?" and a discussion of the difficulties of shopping for a dressy outfit.

Although this kind of chitchat suffices for brief encounters, you don't want to get stuck there. For longer conversations, especially when you sit down at the table, the challenge is to move on to topics that stimulate further discussion. The following suggestions can help you do so.

- **Listen for cues.** Pay attention to information you can follow up on, especially anything related to interests or hobbies. This is important because you can't spend the whole evening talking about the bride and groom. Getting into these topics also gives you an opportunity to bring others into the conversation, which makes it livelier. You can say, "You're into hiking? Where are your favorite trails?" If someone mentions he's a spear-carrier at the opera, don't just say, "Oh," and leave it at that. Ask more about it: "How did you get into that? What's it like?" Did someone mention she just retired? You might ask, "How are you finding your new lifestyle?"

Look for points of similarity you can pick up on, such as "Oh, you're taking a course in classical music? I want to learn more about music, too. Tell me about the class." At one wedding, the person I was talking to taught with the bride, an assistant professor at a university. It was natural to ask, "What subject do you teach?" When the answer was sociology, I mentioned, "My sister is a sociology professor." That led to a small-world experience; the man knew my sister.

On another occasion, I told a wedding guest, "I hear you publish books." It turned out that she specialized in cookbooks, and I learned how to create a successful cookbook.

- **Bring up vacations.** Travel is an ideal topic for social occasions such as weddings, and you can ask someone, "Where did you vacation last?" Wait for the response, and then continue with "What was your experience there?" The point is to show interest in them first and to listen, rather than jump in immediately with "Oh, we've been there, too." Did someone just return from a cruise? Ask about the ports they visited, accommodations, on-board activities, and the other passengers.

  Conversation can be stimulating if people vacation differently from you. Suppose they're partial to rafting down rapids, exploring places like Borneo, or other adventure trips. If that's not your style, you can respond, "I'm too scared to do that. I'd rather play on the beach in Florida." The banter will follow.

- **Talk about the event itself.** Questions like "What do you think of this gorgeous ballroom?" lead people to describe other weddings they've attended. You can also ask, "What was your wedding like?" or "What was the best wedding you ever attended?" Trivia can add interest, as in "Do you know more weddings are performed in Gatlinburg, Tennessee than anywhere else in the United States except Las Vegas?" At a destination wedding, you can also chat about the hotel, the scenery, and interesting side trips.

  Keep the conversation positive, regardless of whom you talk to. If the canapés are soggy and tasteless and the service is terrible, do not mention it. A wedding is not the place for negative comments. Be careful what you say about other people, too. If you're about to comment on the lady walking by in an awful dress, remember that the person next to you may be her sister. You know very little about these people. Be cautious.

- **Connect people.** As you meet guests, you can introduce them to others you've just met, which starts a whole new round of conversation. This helps everyone's social life, including yours. Be sure your introductions provide information that gets people talking, as in "Jerry is a veterinarian in Montana" or "Stephanie grew up in Miami, too."

  When talking to guests who are acquaintances, you already know the basics about them. To draw them out further, you can say, "It's good to see you again. How are you enjoying your time-share in Mexico?" or "Did you ever take that CPR course you mentioned? How was it?" If you can't think of anything, try "What's new in your life?"

Conversations with the Bridal Couple and Family

What do you say to the bride and groom on the receiving line? There are several options, and you'll be relieved to know your comments should be brief. Compliments work every time. Mention the ceremony and/or venue, as in:

- "I thought your vows were wonderful."
- "The minister was so moving [or entertaining]."
- "It was a beautiful ceremony."
- "What a gorgeous place to get married."
- "What a beautiful day you got."
- "I'm so thrilled to be at your wedding."
- "You're a beautiful bride."
- "I'm so glad to meet you at last. I've heard so much about you." (This applies for those times when you've never met the bride or groom.)

The reception is another opportunity to talk to the bride and groom as they make their rounds visiting tables. Compliments work well here, too. Because a great deal of time and attention has been spent on décor, you can always say, "The table looks fabulous. The centerpieces are lovely." Or how about "The wine is superb." Or even "The band is great. I haven't stopped dancing." The couple truly wants to hear what a wonderful time you're having, and a short comment is all that's necessary. If you really want to engage them further, you can also inquire, "When are you leaving on the honeymoon and where are you going?" However, do respect the fact they have many people to chat with. Although they would love to spend time with you, they also have to move on.

At some point you'll undoubtedly talk to the couple's parents, as well. Here you can always say, "John and Patty are

such a wonderful couple. You must be so proud of them."
Other options: "What a warm and beautiful wedding this is,"
or "What a wonderful idea to hold the wedding in Maui [or
Las Vegas]." They'll be happy to hear your appreciation. You
can also welcome in-laws with comments like "It's great that
you're all part of the family" or "Now I can see where Paul
gets his looks and charm," or "You're getting a great son- [or
daughter-] in-law."

When you meet the best man or maid of honor, you can say
(if it's true, of course), "What a moving speech you made."
People tend to feel surprised and pleased when you compliment them. It's always right to thank the bride and groom and
parents for including you and/or to tell them how happy you
are to be there.

Celebrate

Do your best to have a good time. You're going to spend four
or five hours at a typical wedding. The couple and/or their
families have spent a lot of money on this celebration. It's
important to mingle, dance, and help others enjoy themselves.
If you just sit there, you're telling the hosts, "Entertain me."

It's in your own interests to circulate. If you're seated next
to a boor at your table, you may have to get up and table-hop
(or dance more than you planned) to escape. But keep an open
mind, and you never know who will cross your path.

BRIDE AND GROOM

"Brides are concerned about meeting, greeting, and making
guests feel comfortable. They worry, 'Will I remember everyone's name?'" says Antonia van der Meer, editor-in-chief of

Modern Bride. Echoing her words, a new bride told me, "At my wedding I felt shy about going over to people I didn't know, and I didn't know more than half of them." Of course you want to be a good host or hostess, and there are ways to make everyone feel welcome:

- **Check the guest list.** Remember, you drew it up. Read it over to familiarize yourself with names in advance. Since you spent so much time on the seating chart, it's a pretty good bet you know which table seats your father's business associates or your new mate's cousins. If you still forget a name, relax. People understand this is a day filled with excitement and distractions. You're being tugged in many directions and your attention isn't as focused as usual.

  As you glance through the guest list, you can decide in advance whether there are certain people you should seek out. Some may have traveled long distances to attend the wedding and deserve attention, or an elderly or disabled guest may not be able to get up to come to you.

- **Tell them you're glad they attended.** To make people feel special, make eye contact as you speak with them. These statements work well on the receiving line or at the reception: "I'm so glad you could come" or "I'm so happy you could be here" or "It's an honor to have you here." If you know something about the person, it's always appropriate to say, "Michael told me you grew up with him in Pittsburgh [or how much he enjoys working with you]."

  As you table-hop during dinner and visit people strategically, keep in your back pocket thoughtful questions, such as "How was your food?"; "Was your trip here okay?"; and "Have you gotten something to drink yet?" These queries give you something to say to guests, and at the same time make people think, "Wow, she/he is making sure I've eaten and am being taken care of."

- **Arm yourself with escape lines.** As the bride and groom, you are partners in greeting guests—and sometimes you may divide and conquer. The bride may circle the room in one direction and the groom in the other direction. Or you may make the rounds together. Either way, because some guests are chatty, be prepared with escape lines like "My mom is adamant we have to say hello to everyone," or "Dad will kill me if I don't make it around to see my cousins," or "It's been wonderful speaking with you but you can't imagine how many people I haven't managed to see yet." You want to talk to people, but you have to cover a lot of ground. Other guests will be disappointed if you don't make your way around to them, too.

- **Say good-byes.** Good-byes at the end of the wedding are pretty straightforward. Try "I hope you had a wonderful time. Thanks for coming," and "Did you pick up your little gift?" or "Have a safe trip home." For someone special, you might add, "We'll send a postcard from the honeymoon."

    Incidentally, if a guest gets drunk or otherwise behaves badly, ask someone else to handle the person and take him out of the room for a walk. You're the host and hostess. You don't really want to have to deal with such issues. This is your special time. If you have a wonderful time yourselves, so will your guests.

Weddings are a chance to celebrate a couple starting a life together and to share their joy. Thinking about conversation strategies in advance will help you participate, talk to other guests, and enjoy yourself. If you're the bridal couple, try the conversation ideas in this chapter to connect with everyone and glide through your big day.

PART III

BUSINESS AND PROFESSIONAL OCCASIONS

CONFERENCES, CONVENTIONS, MEETINGS

People attend trade shows, symposiums, conventions, meetings, and other professional or business events for all kinds of reasons. These occasions are opportunities to network, meet potential customers, make an initial or ongoing professional impression, gather information, connect with possible employers, or cross-pollinate with peers. And you're likelier to get the results you want when you arrive prepared and focused on what you wish to accomplish. How you spend your time depends on your goal.

TARGETING PEOPLE TO TALK TO

If you want to meet people or learn about industry trends, a key question at a business or professional event is: "Who must I talk to in order to make the event worthwhile?" Even if you know the answer, it's smart to check out the sponsoring organization's Web site in advance for information on the program, guest speakers and panelists, and other likely attendees. Once you know these details, you can prioritize people you want to talk to and think about what you want from them. You can also learn as much as possible about "must-sees."

Remember, you can Google virtually anyone online for background information. The more you know, the more you have to discuss.

WORKING THE ROOM

Whether you're at a reception, a luncheon buffet, or a break from a meeting, it's common to assume that everyone knows everyone else, which isn't true. Many people are there for the same reason you are. They want to connect and learn, and they expect to talk to you. They're often looking for ideas, vendors, professional services, and/or people to partner with for projects.

If it's hard to initiate conversation, take a deep breath to center yourself. Realize you break through a barrier when you make the first move. Glance around the room for someone on your must-see list, or look for a person standing alone and make eye contact. That's almost always a way to make a friend. At a cocktail party, another option is to head for the bar or hors d'oeuvres table, where people tend to assemble, and see what happens.

March up and introduce yourself, as in, "Hello, I'm Frank Jones from Bridge and Hall. And you are?" Because people want to talk about themselves, all you have to do is ask a relevant open-ended question about *them* to get a conversation going. All-purpose openers include these:

- "What brings you here?"
- "What do you hope to get out of this event?"
- "Have you been here before? What has been your experience?"
- "So how did you get into this business [or involved in this professional organization]?"

- "What do you think of the meeting so far?"
- "What are you focusing on now?"
- "What is the biggest challenge you're facing?"
- "What's your experience with [outsourcing or . . .]?"

Or maybe you want to talk to a speaker you heard earlier in the day. You can say, "I'm Joe Wallace at . . . I'm interested to know what you think about . . ." Compliments are always useful tools, as in "That was a terrific presentation you gave." Any speaker loves hearing praise. If you've researched the person's background, this is also a time to use what you've learned, as in "I understand you won the . . . Award last month."

Identification badges offer clues to additional conversation starters. Perhaps someone works for a company you've read about. You might open with, "There's a lot going on at . . . these days," or "Oh, you've got a new CEO." Then pause and wait for the response, which will undoubtedly elaborate on recent changes. Or take another direction with "You're at XYZ Corporation. Do you know George Smith? I used to work with him at . . ." Or you can simply check the badge and say, "Jones Insurance Group. Tell me about it." Often when you start talking, an acquaintance of the person comes over and you make another contact.

Remember, most people want to talk about their business. The more you can get them to discuss who they are and what their needs are, the better they like you and the more positively they view your firm or company.

Mingling is less important if you just want to learn about new research at a meeting. But an event is more enjoyable when you chat with people, and you can pick up valuable information when you least expect it.

COPING WITH NAMES

It's embarrassing to forget someone's name but easy to do when you're meeting lots of new people. Name badges aren't always available. Even if they are, people don't necessarily wear them all the time. What if you see someone you had a great time with at the same event two years ago? It's common to wait to approach the person hoping the name will eventually come to you. Instead, why not walk over with a smile on your face and say, "I remember we met at the Tucson conference. Tell me your name." The other person will say, "Oh yes, I'm . . ." It's very comfortable because you did remember him (and he may not recall your name either).

You're also on the spot when someone comes up to you, says, "Hello, how are you doing?" and you don't recall who the person is. The only way out is to make a funny remark at your own expense, such as "I lost my memory years ago. How do we know each other?"

There are all kinds of tricks to help you remember a name when you're first introduced. The easiest is to repeat the name immediately, as in "It's a pleasure to meet you, Gayle." If you didn't get the name the first time, ask the person to say it again right away. I'd suggest a memory course, if necessary, but I took one a few years ago and when the instructor called one day about a change in schedule, I couldn't remember *her* name.

BREAKING INTO CLUSTERS

A physician who frequently attends radiology meetings confesses, "I'm okay with them except for the cliques of people who know each other. They're hard to crack." Most of us find tight clusters daunting, and there are a few ways to deal with them. One answer is to arrive at an event on time or even a bit early so you can be present as people enter the room—and most importantly, before conversation circles have formed. If you meet a few individuals briefly at that time, you have entrée to approach them later as they chat with others. You can say, "Hello again, Tom," which will almost certainly lead Tom to introduce you to the rest of the group. One way to keep conversation going is to follow up with "How did you all get to know one another?"

Or you might walk up to a cluster, stand there for a minute, and try to make eye contact. Often you'll get noticed and you can say something like, "You look like a friendly group. I'm . . ." Do not, however, intrude on an obviously private conversation.

Accept that sometimes a circle just won't let you in. Usually it's a sign of their insecurity. Confident people with high self-esteem want to reach out to people and say, "Hi, Larry. Come on over." They know they can learn from everyone and that it's stimulating to invite someone new into the conversation.

If clusters are too hard to deal with, take the advice of the physician and stand on line for a drink at the bar. "People are very friendly there, especially if they've already had a martini or two," he reports.

Warmth *can* vary. For example, as a general rule, technical people in an industry tend to be friendlier toward one another than those in management are. One company culture may be hostile toward competitors while another in the same industry welcomes chats with you.

EFFECTIVE SELF-PROMOTION

Attendees at many events expect vendors, exhibitors, and consultants to advertise themselves, and they may be looking for people to hire. Someone may walk over to you and ask, "What do you do?" Do you have a response ready? This is a time to have a thirty-second "elevator speech" ready to roll off your tongue. This script introduces you and quickly describes what is most relevant about you.

An effective speech is not about boasting or aggressively selling yourself. It relies on facts to tell people how impressive you are, as in, "I was a partner at . . . Now I've started a new firm that helps international investors do business here." Or "I help companies get the most out of their dollar when marketing home furnishings."

You want to provide enough information about yourself to be remembered. But when someone you've just met asks about your job or company, respond with a sound bite, not a ten-minute soliloquy. The idea is to answer briefly, then go on to "Tell me about you." One of the key skills of conversation is the ability to step outside yourself and ask, "What does this person really want from this talk?" Nobody wants to hear a monologue on your family or your hobby.

Although your speech should be memorized, it should *sound* natural, rather than rehearsed. Ask a trusted friend or colleague for feedback on your speech and body language. Remember, a smile helps you come across as warm, friendly, and nonthreatening. Check out your handshake, too. Make sure it's firm enough to show you mean business while not being a death grip. Follow with a smooth release of the hand. See page 30 if clammy palms are an issue.

It's great when people seek you out to talk—and it's important to do what you can to encourage approaches. Open body language helps, but props can work, too. For example, dramatic jewelry on a woman attracts attention and gives people a way into conversation. If you own an attractive necklace, wear it. People often comment, "Where did you get it?" Or "You're wearing handsome cufflinks." If there's an interesting story behind the accessory, this is the time to tell it. A special pen can also act as a conversation starter. Someone invariably says, "What an unusual pen. I've never seen a clip in the form of a guitar before."

When the executive director of a trade association attended industry events—and wanted to advertise the group's next convention in Florida—she wore a small Disney pin. People asked questions about the pin, which gave her an opening to talk about the upcoming convention to those who might want to attend.

AFTER-HOURS SOCIALIZING

Business events are also about building relationships. People want to work with people they know—people they trust and feel comfortable with. If attendees socialize after long hours of panels or presentations, you've got a chance to meet more people or strengthen ties with those you've recently met. Everyone wants to unwind at the end of the day, and this is a good time for casual banter and more personal conversation.

Pick up on what someone mentioned earlier. Perhaps you meet an attendee from Ohio while you're having a drink at the bar. You talked to him briefly that morning. A way in is "I've never been to Ohio. Tell me about it." Listen to the response and ask probing follow-up questions to keep conversation rolling.

Ask a fundraiser about the techniques she uses to persuade people to part with their money. Did someone say he had a Fulbright to Bordeaux to study French literature several years ago? It's easy to segue into "How did you get from French literature to the oil and gas industry?" Does a comptroller build furniture in his garage? Ask, "What projects are you working on now?" to get him talking. If an attendee is a volunteer fireman, you can ask about the training or say, "That's such dangerous work. What was the closest call [or the biggest fire] you've had?"

Stay away from politics and religion in your conversations with new acquaintances unless these topics are the focus of the event. Subjects involving values are dangerous because someone turned off by your opinion loses objectivity about your business competence. A consultant told me about a professional function where he starting talking to someone at the bar. "I thought I might want to work with him on a project. But he made one negative comment after another about a nationality. He assumed I would think the same way. Instead his poor judgment and insensitivity turned me off. I lost respect for him. It ruined any chance of our working together."

TABLE TALK

Sometimes a luncheon or dinner follows an awards event or symposium, or a chamber of commerce meeting with a speaker includes a dinner-reception. The dinner table has been a center for conversation through the ages, and it's an important business setting. If seating is not assigned, you can maximize the value of people at your table. Ask someone you met earlier (and want to know better) to sit with you. And why not be the first one at the table to introduce yourself, then ask others to do the same? Act as a "host" to help people interact and exchange information and ideas. Invite everyone in, making eye contact around the table. If you're uncomfortable looking people in the eye, make the time to practice this skill. Without it, you can't connect or establish trust.

Often conversation flows naturally after introductions. If not, bring up relevant topics you've read about in trade publications, as well as *Forbes* or the *Wall Street Journal*. For example, this is a time to bring up those new government regulations everyone is worried about. Someone has to take responsibility to get conversation going, and it shows confidence and professionalism to take the lead. If you sit at dinner and all you get is the speech, you've missed out.

Sometimes bright, interesting people need encouragement to start interacting. I remember sitting at a table with an advertising executive, an economics professor, a financial consultant, and a businessman from Madrid. The question "Where are you from?" led to a discussion of cultural differences in conducting business.

Adaptability is key. Practice becoming a chameleon who can adjust conversation paths depending on the people, and take advantage of what's happening in the moment. At one conference a lawyer overheard someone across the table mention his hobby was ventriloquism. "I hear you're a ventriloquist," he said later. The man proceeded to regale everyone with tidbits about ventriloquist schools and the annual ventriloquist convention. You never know what information you will pick up and where it will go.

CONVENTION ADVICE

At a convention, you may be an exhibitor or an attendee from inside or outside the industry. You may be there to develop new business, learn what you can, or accomplish other goals. Realize the organizers want you to have a productive experience. They want you to come back. If you're a first-timer, you may receive a brightly colored ribbon to wear to identify you to veteran members who can watch out for you and help you navigate. Some organizations may contact you well in advance of your arrival to smooth your way. Whether you've attended before or not, these tips can help:

1. **Scout out people you know.** If you're alone, help yourself feel more comfortable by contacting colleagues from the preconference registration list. Schedule at least one or two evenings with someone you might have met or who has mutual colleagues, or who you know shares interests with you.

2. **Take advantage of helpful functions.** If you want to meet people who can do you some good, always attend networking functions, no matter how tired you may feel. Hopefully the coordinators have put together these gatherings based on their success with previous groups, and you may be surprised.

3. **Move around.** Sit at a different table each day if your goal is making contacts. In addition to conversation openers mentioned earlier in this chapter, you can talk about topics related to the convention location and facilities. Try "What do you think of the spa?" or "Where are the best shopping areas?" or "Where did you go for dinner last night? Would you recommend it?" People also love to be asked for advice or an opinion, as in "What do you think we should do about . . . ?" Attempt to meet at least one new person each session of the day.

4. **Welcome others.** If you're part of a group, invite/encourage attendees who are sitting or standing alone to join your table at each event, and focus on listening rather than talking. If a badge indicates someone is a "guest/spouse," draw the person into the conversation, and be sensitive if the individual doesn't understand topics of industry discussion. Talk about something relevant to them, such as how they spent the day (or plan to spend tomorrow).

5. **Make a good impression.** Some people attend primarily to socialize with old friends—or to party and have a good time. But if you're there to maintain or develop business or to help your career, the impression you make matters a great deal. Use good judgment. It's always wise to drink less than the people around you.

Appropriate attire is also part of your image. Check the convention Web site or organizer for information on proper dress for various convention functions. When in doubt, it's usually better to dress up, rather than down. What you wear conveys confidence, authority, competence, and power—or not. A vendor who attends a coffee industry meeting every year told me, "I'm the only person there who wears a tie, and everyone remembers me."

LEAVING PEOPLE GRACEFULLY

Depending on your objective, you may want to talk to a few important people or make lots of contacts. In the latter case, unless you're at an event that runs for more than a day, you have a very limited amount of time. Use it wisely. When it's time to move on to a discussion with someone else, pick up on one topic you discussed for a transition and mention it specifically to sound real and genuine. You might say, "This discussion about the trade negotiations is so interesting. I want to talk more about it later. You've been very helpful." Or "I want to hear more about risk management, but I have to catch Gary before he leaves. I really enjoyed talking to you."

An elegant way to leave is to introduce the person to a third party. Say something like "I know someone looking for an architect. I'll introduce you." Or "Hey, Betty, I just met Bill here. He works for the *Los Angeles Times* and also loves to skydive." Then you turn and explain to Bill: "Betty works for an entertainment company." People love that.

To prevent any awkward moments at evening events, one businessman parks his car across the street from the hotel or restaurant and avoids valets. "I don't want to be stuck on line with people I just left while I'm waiting for my car, and endure a dreadful fifteen minutes of small talk. When I go, I want to be gone," he told me.

If you feel the conversation starting to wane, make a smooth departure. You don't want the last impression of you to be the awkward three minutes you spent standing next to each other saying nothing and shuffling your feet before one of you slunk away. When you leave people wanting more, they think you are interesting.

Be sensitive to cues, such as eyes that drift as you talk. That's a signal you're losing the person. Respond with, "I don't want to hold you up. Maybe we can follow up on this later." Or "I'd love to hear more about this, but I know you've got a lot of people to talk to." That's a great way to exit on their terms.

Another option is "I'm going to get a drink. Can I get one for you?" People need an out and an opportunity to say no, even if that disappoints you. A "No" probably means they don't want you to return—not because they don't like you, but because it's time to meet others.

ADDING VALUE

When you want to follow up a connection after any event, write a short note by hand saying what a pleasure it was to meet the person. Or pen something like "Dear John, I tried the suggestions you made at the conference. They worked! Hope to see you at the June meeting. Best, . . ."

You can also make yourself useful. Say, "I just saw this article that will interest you. Thought I'd send it along," or "I'm e-mailing that study we spoke about." People love it when you pay attention to them, and acts of generosity are often an investment in the future.

Professional and business events are great places to meet large numbers of valuable people and learn. Even competitors can be helpful. If they like you, they may recommend you down the road when they can't take a project themselves. Remember to bring a large supply of business cards to hand out when people ask, or offer them on your own initiative. You may have to push yourself to circulate or to sit down at a table full of strangers. But it's the way to grow confidence in yourself and get what you want.

BUILDING BUSINESS
RELATIONSHIPS

There's a difference between a passing conversation at a conference and developing a long-term business relationship. Once you've met new contacts, prospective customers, or others who can be helpful to you, the next step is building a personal as well as professional bond. It's this move to another level that differentiates you from everyone else out there. People like to do business with friends, and the rewards can be enormous.

FINDING SIMILARITY

It takes time and subtlety to get to know someone. Conversations can't focus solely on business all the time, and people must feel comfortable enough with you to open up and talk freely. The faster you can find common ground on a personal level, the faster you can start easing into a relationship. If you both went to the same school or grew up in the same area, that's a strong and immediate commonality. When your backgrounds are very different, other points of similarity can give you something besides business to talk about.

Possibilities are all around you when you sharpen your

awareness and look for them. For example, maybe you're both serious athletes. In that case, you can say, "You're training for the triathlon [or going skiing in Utah]? I am, too." Similarity gives you a foundation for trust, which is a basic element in doing business.

Perhaps you drive the same vehicle. You can say, "Oh, you've got a BMW [or a Harley-Davidson]. So do I." Now you can compare experiences and swap information. The same kind of connection occurs when you read the same best-sellers or watch the same TV series or root for the same team. This commonality is "glue" for business or professional relationships. If you're both Chicago Cubs fans, you can always discuss last night's game or last week's trade. The thrill of a win or commiseration in defeat brings you closer together.

Any common interests can be markers for other areas to explore and can suggest subsequent questions. For example, the guy who owns a BMW is likely to be affluent and in a technical, managerial, or professional occupation. He may be a golfer like you, which raises another topic for conversation.

THE ART OF SCHMOOZING

Once you've identified common ground, you have a basis for schmoozing, which is casual chatting about subjects that aren't directly business related. Schmoozing deepens and maintains relationships. It adds a human touch and says, "You're more than just someone I do [or want to do] business with. I value you as a person."

For a tax attorney, schmoozing takes the form of swapping jokes with certain clients every week. It's "Wait till you hear this one." The laughter and camaraderie generated is not only fun, it strengthens his professional relationships. Loyalty and trust grow from these interactions.

Not everyone has the talent (or the interest) for comedy. Some people are raconteurs; others are not. We all have our own style. But there are almost always other areas of commonality you can tap. A consultant schmoozes with a CEO she meets with regularly. Before they get down to business, they often share stories about their toddlers, discussing strollers and car seats. You might remember that a potential client just had a child. Ask him, "How is the baby doing?"

The point is to establish a pattern of relaxing, affable interchange that both of you enjoy. Athletes can schmooze about anything from equipment to sports injuries to personal trainers. For many people, food is a point of connection. If you'd both walk a mile for good barbecue or Asian food, you have the basis for bonding on one level. You can reminisce about memorable meals and talk about new restaurants and regional differences in recipes. You also have a built-in excuse to go out to dinner together. If you're both active at church or interested in nature photography, you have something personal to talk about anytime you meet.

BRING WHATEVER YOU KNOW

As you get to know someone, you gradually learn more about the person's life and family. You can take the information with you whenever you meet and refer to previous conversations. Did someone mention his daughter competes in gymnastics? When you see him again, you can say, "Tell me about Melanie's latest competition." Everyone is proud of their children's accomplishments. Who doesn't want to crow about them? Listen attentively, and the person will bask in your interest, then walk away thinking, "What a great guy [or gal]." Maybe a client's son played the lead in a school production.

Remember to ask, "How was the show?" With practice, you can automatically tune in to meaningful topics that fit the person and situation.

Make a note that someone is building a deck on his house or adding a pool. Anytime you talk to the person, you can ask, "How is the work progressing?" Perhaps the child of an important contact is having an operation soon. Remind yourself to say, "Good luck with Peter's surgery," when you see the person next week. Thoughtfulness is remembered, and that's one of the ways you nurture a relationship.

One of my favorite all-purpose lines is "Did you have any luck . . . ?" It's "Did you have any luck finding a used car for your son online [or buying a sports watch]?" Or "Did you have any luck hiring a new nanny [or a wallpaper hanger]?"

Perhaps a contact sold a condo, only to have the buyer back out. You can demonstrate empathy with "Oh no! What a disappointment." You might follow up with "What's your next step?"

Does someone play the clarinet in a band on weekends? Why not inquire, "How did the band get started?" or "Where are you playing next?" Ask a rower, "Were you on the crew team at school? How did you get into it?" Or "What keeps you rowing now?"

Or maybe a client is talented at needlepoint. You can say, "How do you choose your pillow designs?" Or "What is it about needlepoint that grabs you so?" In the course of conversation she may reveal a deep dark secret: she's always wanted to own a needlepoint store. Add the information to your list of conversation options to bring up next time you meet.

The goal is to engage people so they want to do business with you or see you later. They meet many people every day, but if you build a connection, they remember you.

Searching for Clues

When you're in someone's office to pitch a product or program, look for clues to subjects you can chat about before you talk business. Pay attention to photos on display. If a picture on the desk shows the person shaking hands with a senator, you want to know how that happened. Family photos and children's drawings on the wall reveal a lot about marital status and parenting interests. You can comment, "I see you've got three soccer players in the family," which will lead him to talk about the kids' activities. These kinds of conversations help you feel relaxed with each other and weave a bond.

For additional information, subtly listen in when the phone rings. As the person talks, you may learn that his back went out over the weekend and an ambulance delivered him to the emergency room on a board. After the call, you can make a sympathetic comment and show concern, as in "That must have been painful." People love to talk about their health problems to willing listeners, and next time you meet, you can follow up with "How's your aching back?" Sincere attention to personal details helps strengthen the relationship.

When the Customer Comes to You

In some fields or businesses, such as retail stores, beauty salons, spas, or even medicine, the customer goes to the place of business. If there are no photos on the wall or other clues to conversation topics, you can ask a question like "How did your weekend go?" Such chitchat demonstrates interest in the individual. When you make it a regular routine, you can learn a lot about someone and build customer loyalty.

In fact, ignore such small talk at your peril. One woman left her physical therapist because he treated her like a pair of knees. "He never said, 'How are you?' or tried to make a connection," she says. "I was lying there in pain, and he kept talking to a coworker about a movie he saw." And once I had a fitness trainer who talked constantly about himself and *his* weekend. He drove me to switch to someone else.

At the same time, do be sensitive to the fact that some people are very private and prefer not to talk about themselves. If someone gives one-word answers or stares out the window, take the hint.

Out-of-the-Office Occasions

A very successful businessman once told me, "If you really want to understand what clients' issues are, go out together and have drinks or a meal. That's where they open up and tell you, 'My boss is driving me nuts. I can't get done what I need to get done. How do I handle it?'"

The most relaxed and personally revealing conversations usually take place outside the office. Why? Because there are all those interruptions at work. People walk in and out. The phone rings. There's a meeting in twenty minutes. In contrast, a client can take it easy at breakfast; the day hasn't started yet. He can tell you what's in his heart over pancakes. Maybe he's worried about his girlfriend's new job and his own career. If you simply listen and speak only when he says, "What do you think?" you behave like a friend and cement a personal bond.

Everyone eats lunch and everyone likes to be taken out to lunch. If you can afford it, treat someone important to you. In my business, I often interview experts, and I recently took an expert on Japan out to lunch. I got to know him by asking questions like "How did a guy from Michigan get interested in Japan and wind up living in Tokyo?" I also found out that he loves sushi. The next time I saw him, I could ask about his favorite sushi restaurants. You can file such tidbits in your head, or better yet put them on a Rolodex card so you won't forget them.

The same strategy works well at dinner or drinks at the end of the day. A martini, a bottle of wine, and people start to talk. Then you find out how you can help them or how they can help you. However, subtlety is crucial. Understand they're there to have dinner and want to feel comfortable. First you can start with something like "How's the family?" or "How did your vacation go?" Eventually you lead the conversation to the business you want to discuss. No one wants to be swamped by aggressive salespeople.

To move along relaxed conversation, one man always reads the newspaper "Week in Review" section. "It gives you everything that happened that week, and you know enough to have a point of view and be able to talk knowledgeably," he says. You can also pick up on other issues you discussed the last time you met, as in "How did your office move go?" Or "I read in Crain's that you got the . . . account after all. What a coup. Congratulations."

Golf Outings. People love golf as a business setting—even if they're terrible golfers—because it's quiet, removed from the office, and the golfers are trapped together for about four hours engaging in a pursuit both enjoy. No other activity offers these attractions, and relationships are forged here.

When you play golf with a client or contact, you can start off with the subject of the kids and "What did you do last week?" If the weather is balmy, you can mention the article you read on golfers in Calcutta playing in 110-degree heat. Because you have plenty of time to cover the business on your mind, you can proceed at a leisurely pace. You're forced to take a conversation break when you tee off, and have time to collect your thoughts.

A commercial real estate broker told me, "I usually begin by asking how their business is doing, rather than mentioning my business. I've also found low key is best. Sometimes I play with prospective customers or it's a case where actual business never panned out. I don't believe in being in someone's face and I never say, 'How come we're not doing more business?' I'm good at what I do and people like me. The information will come out naturally over four hours."

Parties. A customer's Christmas party is an opportunity to raise your visibility and talk to people who can give you additional business or help you in other ways. Heavy-duty business conversation isn't appropriate, but you can ask a general question like "How is the new plant in Mexico?" You can also talk about holiday plans and New Year's resolutions or chat about vacations. If a client recently vacationed in Aruba, you can say, "Hey, where did you stay? We're thinking about taking a break. Are there any side trips you'd suggest when we get tired of lying on the beach?" People feel intelligent and powerful when asked for advice.

These are times to expand and strengthen relationships, as long as you use good judgment. It's a good idea to make the drink you're carrying last the whole party.

Any event has a social aspect if it takes place outside the office, and there are times when you're invited to a business-connected birthday party or wedding. You may be seated at a table full of people who do business with your company. Just remember this is a social occasion, and keep conversation low key and subtle. But there may be opportunities to network and follow up. For example, you might send someone an article pertaining to a topic you discussed.

Pay attention to the spouse of an important tablemate. Because most people have children, one consultant asks, "Do you have kids? Tell me about them." If the spouse has a career, he switches the conversation to that subject. "People appreciate the interest and remember you," he says.

INTERNATIONAL SAVVY HELPS

Globalization means you may be meeting and conducting business with people from other countries either here in the United States or while traveling abroad. In or out of the office, lack of knowledge of cultural differences can make you look foolish and even affect the outcome of contracts and deals. For example, Americans regularly ask questions, but someone from Japan may view questions as intrusive. A firm handshake works here, but not in all countries. Some cultures consider it rude to make eye contact or to disagree.

To avoid misunderstandings and other potential potholes, learn in advance all you can about the country involved. Begin with simple geography. Keep some conversation topics in mind for chatting at dinners or elsewhere.

Sports are an excellent subject to raise in most situations, as in, "Tell me about [name of country's] most popular sports star." Ask about the nation's cuisine and request advice on dishes to try. The country's history is another possible topic. For detailed help with international etiquette and specific cultures, see page 148 for resources.

WORKING ON LISTENING SKILLS

People reveal more about who they really are when they feel you understand them. To reach that level, most of the time you need to pay attention and listen, which is what great leaders do. "If you're out with a new client and keep your mouth shut, as you leave the person will say, 'That was a great meeting.'

People love to hear themselves talk. I listen eighty percent of the time," says a consultant to Fortune 500 companies.

However, he had to learn to keep quiet. Some promising executives have trouble listening, too. They could have learned a lot from my father. When I was growing up, he had a second job at night selling Cutco knives door-to-door. Around 7 p.m. he pushed away from the dinner table, grabbed his sample case, and headed out for his first call. His customers didn't have much money. Yet he sold them sets of carving knives that cost hundreds of dollars. These people had more important places to spend their cash. They bought knives from my father because he listened to them, made return calls, and was interested in their lives. A few became lifelong friends.

Do remember, however, that it also takes input from you to establish rapport. It's important to loosen up and share something of yourself. You don't have to be in your "lawyer mode" or your "banker mode" all the time. Just be aware of boundaries. Appropriate personal revelation depends on the situation. If a CEO has two children he talks about, and you have kids yourself, why *not* mention them and compare notes on coaching teams? Just make sure his family takes center stage, not yours. Be careful to avoid "one-upmanship" in this or any other area. No one feels good when it's practiced on them. You build relationships through positive interactions, not negative ones.

Remember, too, that business-related friendships are different from social ones; you must maintain a positive image. Beware of disclosing personal information that could reflect negatively on you or your business. Ask yourself, "What do I want the person to know about me?" It is inappropriate to talk with a new customer about your marital problems or the messy details of your divorce. If you get too personal, you can scare people away.

Incidentally, self-disclosure doesn't have to involve personal information about you. It could be your opinion of the keynote speaker at an event you both attended, as in "I thought she was dynamic" or "He was entertaining, but I felt he didn't have much new to say." This is especially effective if you're trying to draw out an introvert, someone who is not naturally comfortable in conversation. Your view of a cultural event (as in "I loved the play. It transported me") is another form of self-disclosure where you invite another opinion by providing the person with something to respond to. In such cases, you must be willing to offer information about yourself in a way that makes it okay for someone to disagree with you—and be open to hearing a conflicting view. The other person has to feel comfortable responding to your opinion with his/her own, as in "I had a different experience. The play dragged for me."

"Health talk lite" is also a good way to bond. If someone tells you about a knee injury, you might mention, after you've listened, "I threw my knee out on the treadmill myself. It's taking months of exercises to get back to near normal again." You might even recommend a book on knee exercises that helped you. Just be careful about issuing unasked-for advice. That could create tension.

THE VALUE OF FAVORS

Another way to build trust is to assist people. Maybe someone tells you, "My son is looking for an internship in investment banking." If you know people in that field, you can say, "I may be able to help. I'll e-mail some friends and contacts and see what's available." Many successful individuals match people up with each other and are facilitators of relationships.

If someone has a great screenplay, they offer, "I know a TV producer who might be interested. I'll check."

You can notify people of events that will interest them or help them get tickets. You don't go to that trouble with the expectation you'll get something out of it. You just do it. Kindnesses build a foundation for friendship.

People who keep up meaningful relationships tell me that someone who considers you a friend can become a customer years later, or refer other people to you, help you get crucial data, or make it easier to do your job. If you spend time online getting information about colleges for someone's daughter, your effort is going to be appreciated and people will want to reciprocate. Often they want to do a bigger favor for you because nobody wants to owe anything.

Relationships give you an edge in winning business and getting your job done well. Later they promote loyalty to you and your firm or company. In turbulent times, friendships can help keep an account firmly in your hands, despite wooing from competitors. In other cases, a contact today can lead to a contract in the future. Such special relationships develop through personal connection. Someone meets you and thinks, "Oh, I like this person." It's because you're able to make him/her feel comfortable and safe. Some people who do business together eventually get to be hanging-out buddies and/or socialize out of the office.

11

JOB INTERVIEWS

Job interviews are inherently stressful because you don't have a great deal of control. Someone else asks most of the questions and then decides who gets hired. But there is a lot you can do to present yourself optimally. Beyond qualifications and education, employers are looking for confidence, energy, and the ability to answer interview questions and fit in with the organization. To stand out from other candidates, prepare yourself in advance and find ways to connect with the interviewer.

EFFECTIVE RESEARCH

At any job interview you're essentially being asked, "Tell me about you, but also what you know about us." The more you know about the company, the more you have to talk about, the more confident you feel, and the easier it is to build rapport with the interviewer. You can find relevant information on most companies online. For example, personnel changes offer clues to whether an organization grows from within or hires outside the industry.

Check www.vault.com for background on thousands of organizations. You can browse profiles and insider information on company culture, salaries, and diversity in industries ranging from aerospace to fashion to banking. Such details are good indicators of how successful you'll be in the organization. See www.hoovers.com for information on companies, industries, and executives, and try www.zoominfo.com for company intelligence, as well. All of these sites can be used free of charge.

LexisNexis (www.lexisnexis.com) is another online resource for company, industry, market, and legal news. There is a charge for LexisNexis, but free access is often available at the local library.

To understand financials, look at the company's annual report, which is frequently posted on its Web site. Or check the Web site of Investor Relations Information Network (IRIN) at www.irin.com for free access to electronic annual reports and other company information. You want to know where the company is, where it was, and where it's heading. This information is likely to come in handy during your interview.

People you know may be able to provide nuggets of valuable information for the interview, as well. "If you're at Colgate Palmolive and you want to go to Procter & Gamble, network with friends at P&G and with alumni of your college to learn what they're looking for," says Kenneth Arroyo Roldan, a partner at the global executive search firm Battalia, Winston International. "It's no different from applying courtship strategies. If you want to date someone across the room, you'll ask a friend who knows the person for information. Do the same when you're interested in a company."

Roldan finds many junior applicants are better prepared for interviews than senior people because they're accustomed to researching—and they're scared. Seasoned executives, to their detriment, are often overconfident and cocky, he says.

As you prepare, find out all you can about the person who

will interview you, too. Try Googling the individual for education and employment background and useful personal information. Then you can look for points of similarity between you that you might talk about. Is the person a sports fan or a theatergoer? Do you share the same alma mater? Linkage on a personal level can help overcome less-than-perfect qualifications, such as when you have six out of eight credentials the employer is looking for. A simpatico interview assures the interviewer that he/she is making the right hiring choice.

NAVIGATING THE INTERVIEW

It's only human to feel anxious about a job interview when you're worried about questions you'll face and how you will answer them. The reality is interviews can be laced with landmines. You can help yourself feel more secure by writing down every difficult question you can think of. Then prepare responses and practice them beforehand. Be ready to handle requests like "Tell me about yourself." Too many applicants give a thirty-minute soliloquy when the interviewer wants a snapshot. As a general rule, limit your answers to two minutes or less. That's longer than you think.

Candidates also talk too much when answering questions like "Tell me three positive things coworkers will say about you." After responding, there's a temptation to add, "On the negative side . . ." But nobody asked you for negatives. Why volunteer "I don't have much experience in this area"? Talk only about what you do have.

At some point, an interviewer will ask, "Do you have any questions?" Make sure you're armed with a few, such as, "What are the biggest challenges today at Lynch & Partners?"

No amount of preparation is foolproof, of course. You may still have to field an unanticipated question like "Tell me something that will make me remember you as you walk out the door" or "Is there anything I didn't ask you that I should have asked you?" The latter is your opportunity to clarify and expand on an answer that might have left a negative impression. Remember that unexpected questions may be deliberate ploys to test your performance under pressure. The best response is to be as honest and genuine as you can.

Listening is a big part of interviewing, but many job candidates make the common mistake of responding too quickly. If the interviewer mentions, "We're having a lot of trouble with our databases," applicants often jump in with an answer. Your first instinct might be the instant response "I can fix that for you." Yet rushing in gives the impression you're not paying attention to the interviewer. An effective response is, "That can be very frustrating. Can you tell me more about it?" This approach lets interviewers know they've been heard. If you don't understand active listening (see pages 22–23), read more about it.

Another statement that says, "I hear you" is "From what we've talked about, it sounds like you're looking for . . ." This also gives the person a chance to clear up anything you may have misunderstood.

MATCH CONVERSATION STYLE

In general, three factors affect an employer's decision to hire: (1) Can you do the job? (2) Do they like you? (3) Can they afford you? Stellar qualifications may not get you an offer if you haven't connected and demonstrated you're the type of person the company is looking for.

"I coach a lot of people going into the FBI, and they want someone they wouldn't mind sitting with in a car for eight hours," says Carole Martin, president of InterviewCoach.com.

"People think they get jobs strictly on their knowledge-based skills and educational experience. In fact, there's a lot going on about fit."

To show you fit in, try to generate relaxed conversation back and forth. (This is another reason not to give a long speech about yourself, which cuts off two-way communication.) The goal is to leave the interviewer feeling in tune with you and thinking, "I really like this candidate. This person would work out well here."

If you're prepared, you can draw on your knowledge of the company and even chat about a recent article on industry growth in the business press. If the organization is eco-friendly, you might show interest in its efforts to save energy. You could comment on the impressive building or offices.

Maybe you've discovered through research that you have something in common with the interviewer. Bring it up. One TV host first broke into radio when he learned the head of the station loved airplanes. The host, who had been a Navy flier, spent much of the interview discussing aircraft—and got the job. On the other hand, be flexible and ready to "read" the interviewer. Some people aren't interested in small talk and want to get down to business.

The point is to "match" the person across the table and demonstrate you're on the same wavelength. For example, it's important to match pacing of speech to avoid awkwardness between you. If the interviewer talks slowly, you talk slowly. If she talks fast, you talk fast. When you're out of sync, adjust your pace accordingly.

Pay attention to personality, too, and match it. Is an interviewer the effervescent type? Don't sit there in your serious mode and break a connection. People like *you* when you're like *them*. There may be times when you're interviewed by two people. You may connect with one person and not the other.

Try to pay attention to both because sometimes the senior person relies on the subordinate's opinion, or both people may contribute to the hiring decision.

BODY LANGUAGE ISSUES

One of the questions recruiters and human resources people ask themselves is "Does this applicant have the energy and enthusiasm to do the job?" Energy signifies strength and motivation. Employers look for it even for technical jobs where you sit at a computer all day. Do you look interested in getting the job? Or are you bored discussing it?

You communicate energy nonverbally as soon as you arrive at the reception area. One way to do it is to stand as you wait for the interview. Then the interviewer's first impression of you is walking forward. Hold your head up and pull your shoulders up and back. A bit of a bounce in your walk conveys confidence. Shake hands firmly. Make eye contact and smile—at least at first. The objective is to appear friendly as well as confident, motivated, and competent.

MIND YOUR MANNERS

Interviews are difficult enough without sabotaging yourself. Even if you sail through questions, you can be hurt badly by noticeable lapses in etiquette and judgment. Keep these tips in mind:

- Be on time. This may seem too basic to mention, but even people applying for top positions have been known to keep interviewers waiting.
- Turn off your cell phone unless you want to turn off the interviewer.

- Know the difference between confidence and self-importance.
- Avoid drinking coffee or water. Liquids can spill.
- Keep hands free. Put down your briefcase or handbag. Fumbling calls attention to clumsiness. Do not fidget.
- Dress appropriately and be well groomed. A first impression, once made, can be difficult to alter.
- Don't interrupt.
- Don't boast.
- Avoid making negative comments about your current (or previous) employer.

Most hiring decisions are made very quickly, before you've said much of anything. The rest of the interview is spent confirming that first impression. Rehearse with a friend who can be objective and offer constructive advice on your performance. If you're overly nervous, try some calming exercises, such as deep breathing. Visualize a successful interview, and practice, practice, practice what you want to say.

Always follow up an interview with a thank-you note the next day. Many people don't, which is why *you* should. A note demonstrates your good manners, reminds the person of you, and helps you stand out. Try something like, "Thank you for meeting with me yesterday. This position is just what I'm looking for. I know I can make a contribution at [name of company]. Sincerely, . . ."

PART IV

OTHER TIMES FOR CONVERSATION

(12)

DIFFICULT SITUATIONS

Crisis comes in many guises. Someone's loved one dies. A marriage dissolves. Serious illness or economic catastrophe strikes. Challenges in life happen every day, and when they happen to a friend, neighbor, or coworker—anyone you know—it's human to feel inadequate and confused about what to say. In some cases, you may even feel tempted to avoid the individual. But ducking down another aisle at the supermarket doesn't help anybody, and it makes you feel bad about yourself.

There are better, kinder ways to handle sensitive encounters. Start by focusing on the person who is suffering, rather than on your discomfort.

SERIOUS ILLNESS

"A friend of mine has been diagnosed with a rare disease and has been told she has six months to live. I haven't picked up the phone because I don't know what to say to her. I feel like an awful person, and the longer I wait, the harder it is to call."

The colleague who confided this dilemma to me is a very caring woman, and perhaps you can identify with her reaction. The more frightening the diagnosis, the more awkward it can feel to talk to the patient. Yet there is always an appropriate way to show concern and sincerity in the most desperate situations: Be yourself and say what you feel. Tell the truth, as in "I put off calling you because I don't know what to say." That statement validates the enormity of what has happened and opens the door to honest conversation. If you wish, you can add, "This is so terrible, so unfair" or "I can't believe this is happening." A pause afterward gives the person time to respond with something like "Neither can I."

After simple authentic words are said, it's best to keep quiet, listen to what the person wants to talk about, and follow his or her lead. For example, in the case above, conversation might center on how the patient is coping and how the family is taking the news.

Most illnesses have a more hopeful prognosis, although any grave diagnosis stirs dread in our hearts despite treatment advances. You'll feel less anxious when you realize you can always say to a patient, "I'm sorry you have to go through this." Wait for the response. People need to talk about what has happened, about their fears and the emotional trauma they're experiencing. When you listen attentively, you help the person feel understood.

Beware of allowing your own distress to rush you into filling any silence. It is then that it's easy to get into trouble and you risk blurting out something inappropriate. Do not interrupt the patient with a story about someone else you know, unless it's to say, "She found a support group that was helpful." This conversation is about the individual you're talking to, nobody else.

If you wish to offer help, listen to clues to what the person wants and needs. It may be tangible aid, such as kids picked up at school or transportation to treatment. To volunteer, you can say, "I'll take Michael to soccer practice, or would you rather I do something else?" Or "Can I bring dinner over?"

It's easy to say, "Feel better fast," when someone has gallbladder surgery, but other words are required in situations such as heart failure or stroke. Statements like "This must be rough" or "How are you managing?" can open the door to important talk. These are also appropriate statements when you meet the caretaking spouse of someone with Alzheimer's disease. Another option is "How are you holding up?"

When someone is recovering well from a heart bypass, you can say, "It's good to see you up and around." You can also look at your points of connection. If the patient is in your monthly poker group, tell him everyone misses him and awaits his return. Fill him in on winners and losers in the latest game, and whose bluff did or didn't work.

In cases of surgery, you might say beforehand, "I'll be thinking about you as you go in for the operation." For someone close, you might add, "I send you a bear hug." During recovery at home, it's comforting to hear from a friend, "Call me anytime you need me, day or night." People need a support system.

FUNERALS

Funerals or memorial services are probably the most difficult social experiences in our society, in which nobody wants to think about, let alone talk about, death. Yet you usually have time to plan what you might say to the bereaved.

"I'm so sorry" is always appropriate to say, and it is often enough. People think they have to say more, but that isn't true, especially if you don't know the bereaved very well. A gentle touch on the shoulder or arm is a comforting gesture and one that's accepted by most people. Just being there at the moment says a lot.

Any further conversation should depend on your connection to the people involved. If your link is to a bereaved coworker who lost an elderly parent—and there is time to talk—you might inquire, "What was your mother like?" A listening ear conveys caring and concern, and nodding your head at times says you understand. It's important for the bereaved to tell their story. It's part of the healing process.

If you're a close relative or friend of the mourner, you're in a position to say, "How hard this must be," and even hug and cry with the person if you're moved to do so. There is also value in silence and comfort in a simple human presence. Often nothing can be said that makes a difference.

If your connection is to the deceased, it is appropriate to reminisce about the person. You can say, "I have such fond memories of . . ." to the widow, widower, or grieving children. Perhaps the deceased was a friend of yours who happened to be a great volleyball player. You might say, "I'll never forget the time we were down and Ron was in there cheerleading and telling us, 'Come on, everyone. Let's do it.' We wound up winning the game because of him. He was so positive." Such memories are emotional nourishment for those left behind, who may nod their heads and add, "Yes, he was like that."

You give a great gift to a mourner when you say, "He was such a swell guy, and what a sense of humor! I loved being around him." And if the person made a difference in your life, say so, as in, "Bob was a terrific lawyer. He saved me so many times in tough situations. I'll miss him so much."

Whatever your relationship, do not say to the widow or widower, "You're going to be fine." That can make people very angry because they don't feel fine at the moment. Avoid "I know how you feel" for a similar reason. You don't know how someone else feels.

When milling around with others who are paying their respects, you may wish to strike up a conversation. At the funeral of a client where you don't know many people, feel free to ask, "How are you connected to [name of deceased]?" After they respond, they'll undoubtedly ask in return, "How did you know her?" As you chat, you may discover more in common.

If you're close to the family, you may wish to ask the bereaved before the funeral, "How can I be helpful? What do you need?" Because you could be wrong, don't make assumptions. For example, one woman debated about flying in for a funeral because she'd have to make a quick "hit and run" trip. She thought the bereaved would prefer she made a longer visit later. In fact, they needed her then. Remember, this is about what *they* want, which can be different from what you'd want if you were in the family's place.

If it's difficult to express yourself in conversation, you can do so in a condolence note. Write promptly after hearing the news and keep it short. A few lines can be powerful, as in, "I felt so sad to hear about your father's death. He was kind to me on so many occasions, and I will miss him. I send my sincere condolences." Another option that works anytime is "My heart and thoughts are with you and your family at this time of sorrow. I extend my deepest sympathy."

Many people know enough to say, "I'm sorry," at an initial meeting with the bereaved. It's at the next encounter that they feel tongue-tied. Mourners often complain, "People don't talk to me because they don't know what to say. The loss is there, but it's like the elephant in the room."

It's a kindness to acknowledge the loss and reach out. If you meet on the elevator at work, in the cafeteria, or on the street, it's appropriate to greet the person with "How are you doing? I haven't talked to you in a while." Or "This must be a difficult time." Or "How is it going?" These words show empathy and give the person a chance to respond, "I'm okay" or "I don't want to talk about it" or "It's hard." In the latter case, you can say, "I'm sorry." If you know the person well, you can ask, "What's your biggest challenge?" or if you wish, "I wonder whether you've considered a bereavement group."

Realize, too, that mourning goes on for a very long time, even years. If you know the anniversary of a death is approaching (or here), say so with something like "It seems impossible a year has gone by since Larry died." Some people fear that such a statement will "remind" the person of sadness. In fact, the bereaved are well aware of the anniversary. It means a lot that you remembered, too.

DIVORCE

Picture yourself meeting an acquaintance who's been divorced or separated. Would you stop and chat without mentioning the split? Many people do exactly that because they don't want to be nosy and they think they're showing respect. The reality is ignoring the news leaves the other person feeling awkward and wondering whether you know or not—and what you are thinking. Not saying something makes the discomfort worse.

The appropriate script depends in part on your relationship with the person. You don't have to say much—just "I heard you're getting divorced. I'm sorry to hear that." That's enough, unless the person continues talking. It's how the person responds to "I'm sorry" that should guide you in what to say next. If the answer is a one-word yes, you can change the subject. Should the person become teary, you can say, "It must be painful." You might add, "Would it help to talk about it?" when it's a friend. Be aware, however, that some people are happy the relationship is over. Don't assume you know who initiated the divorce.

A sincerely meant, "Is there anything I can do to help?" is a question that opens a door. The person will probably say no. But at least you show consideration and interest. If you're divorced yourself, you can have special value because you know what the experience is like. You may have important information to offer, such as the name of a good divorce lawyer.

You can also provide support as a confidant and buddy to do things with, perhaps a playmate on the dreaded weekend when everyone else seems to be a couple.

Divorce is final. It's over (in the majority of divorces!). But be very careful about what you say in the case of separation. The person may make all sorts of complaints about the marriage and the spouse and look for your support. You may feel tempted to voice your own thoughts, such as, "I always felt you could do better than George." Then they patch it up and three months later may be upset with you. To play it safe, be empathetic but say nothing negative that might come back to bite you. Your words could backfire if the couple gets back together.

JOB LOSS

"I was on the bus today with a guy who was forced to resign. He obviously wanted to vent about how badly he had been treated, and that's important for someone who has been fired," says a hotel industry consultant. He sat quietly as the man told his story. At the end of the bus ride, the man turned to him and said gratefully, "Thanks for listening, man."

Being a good and empathetic listener (instead of fixating on what you're going to say next) is extremely valuable when someone has lost a job. There is not only financial loss for the person, but loss of identity, especially for men, and loss of status and self-esteem. A statement like "That must have been very difficult for you" shows you understand. If you're a friend, you could also ask a bit about the details, as in "What were the circumstances surrounding it?"

People take the loss personally, even when business conditions caused the layoff. They wonder, "What was it about me?" Often you can help put what happened into a larger context with something like "It doesn't sound like it was about you personally, but about a business decision. This market affected lots of people. You have so many skills to offer."

Many people feel awkward and assume the only way to give real help is to say, "Why don't you give me your résumé? Maybe I know a couple of people I can send it to." That relieves *your* anxiety, even though such efforts rarely result in interviews. The recipients of the résumé are likely to respond, "Great candidate, but we're not hiring."

Instead, the best way to ease this transition and support someone is to open up your network of contacts and help the individual connect with other people. For example, if the person is in the transportation industry, you can say, "I know some people in transportation. Maybe you'd like to talk to them. I don't know if they have any jobs available, but you might be able to make a connection to network with someone." That's a gift to someone in a job search.

A career consultant told me, "People tend to think they can only help if they know the same type of people in the same type of industry, but that's a misunderstanding. Everybody is connected to other people. You might know people through your church or your kids' school who have different occupations and lifestyles. You're sharing relationships to help somebody, but you're not promising the world. It's within your comfort level."

What if a friend is fired for cause? Try to find compassion. You might say, "It sounds like there was a disconnect there" or "Maybe the job wasn't the right fit." Talk about what might be learned from the experience. You might add, if appropriate, "Maybe it doesn't feel like it now, but it's going to make you better at what you do."

Incidentally, if you've been laid off yourself in the past and have learned something from the experience, you're in a unique position to be helpful. On more than one occasion a consultant has found himself chatting with someone at a party and asking, "What do you do?" When the reply is, "I just got downsized," the consultant responds, "Well, congratulations. I was downsized, too, and it was the best thing that ever happened to me." Invariably, the laid-off person wants to know all about the other's experience and how he launched his own business. The consultant also goes on to ask, "What's the niche you're going after? What have you got set up?" He told me, "This kind of conversation gives people possibilities. You make their day better in the process."

A circle of family and friends helps put the pieces back together after a divorce, a death, or other personal or economic crisis. In any difficult situation, the answer to "What can I say?" lies within you. When you reach into your heart for kindness and offer relevant information in a nonthreatening way, you provide effective support.

$$\left(\begin{array}{c}13\end{array}\right)$$

TEACHING CHILDREN
CONVERSATION SKILLS

I grew up in a home where everyone sat down at the dinner table each night and talked about their day. When it was someone else's turn, we listened and commented. Although at other times we were hardly a Norman Rockwell portrait, at dinner we exchanged information and support. It was only as an adult that I grew to appreciate the enormous benefits of those nightly conversations. They not only bonded us as a family, but also taught my siblings and I invaluable social skills. I continued the tradition when I had my own children, who became quite comfortable talking to people.

The fact is children receive a gift for life when you encourage them to express themselves and teach them how to empathize and listen to others. These are skills that inspire self-confidence and help youngsters navigate in the world.

YOUNG CHILDREN

You can start teaching conversation skills from the time your child is born. "Young children are capable of more than parents realize. There's a lot going on in their brains, which are firing away. When you interact with babies at birth, their brains make all kinds of connections," says Danielle Kassow, Ph.D., an early childhood researcher who evaluates early learning programs for the nonprofit organization Thrive by Five Washington.

"Start communicating with an infant and you're having an early conversation. When the baby coos or babbles—and you coo or babble back—there's learning going on," she explains. The infant learns the sounds of language, that you take turns when communicating, and that you look people in the eye as you talk to them. Because these skills must be reinforced over and over again, it's important to spend a lot of time talking face to face to babies throughout the day.

To encourage a rich linguistic vocabulary, try to vary the words you use to describe objects to your child. For example, a toddler may say, "That's a ball." A helpful response goes beyond "Yes," to "Yes, that's a red ball and that red ball bounces. We use that ball to play games. Do you want to play a game together?" Although it may take practice, expanding your responses in this way increases vocabulary and helps children learn conversation skills. Learning is not about flash cards or fancy DVDs, but about one-to-one interactions with your child.

Continue talking to your child every chance you get at preschool age when conversation becomes more sophisticated. As youngsters learn more language, ask about their experiences, as in "What did you do today?"; "What did you have for lunch?"; and "What did you do with your friends?" Tell them about your day.

Storybooks are excellent conversation tools. For example, you can choose books with many different characters for preschoolers, which exposes them to a variety of conversations. Different conversations serve as examples children can imitate.

As you read a book to your child, ask open-ended questions

such as, "What do you think happens next?" Ask children, beginning at around age four, to make up their own endings to stories. Such techniques encourage descriptive language and stimulate imagination.

Realize that children aren't able to pronounce language perfectly until around age seven or older. When they mispronounce words, such as saying "rabba" instead of "rabbit," the best response is "Yes, that's a rabbit." Repeat what they say, but correctly. As children keep hearing a word said properly, they eventually learn to pronounce it. This is called modeling, and modeling is not criticism.

Children are taught about listening in preschool, such as when the teacher says, "Everybody be quiet." But you can train your child to listen at home, as well. One way to do it is to help him or her listen to instructions. You might say, "We're going to play a game now. Remember everything I tell you. First I want you to go to the kitchen. Then you're going to get a cup and put it in a saucer," and so forth. Gradually you can increase the number of instructions.

Children need others to listen to them, as well. Invite friends over frequently, especially if you have an only child. Then you can say "Karen, tell Billy something great about his drawing." Billy listens. Then ask Billy to tell Karen something positive about her artwork.

Talking with your youngster helps cognitive and social-emotional growth, and the parent-child relationship. If you can't be home all day, you can use other opportunities to talk with your child as much as possible. Chat on the way to day care or the babysitter or on the way home. Talk during bath time and while preparing for bed. Allow children to help you in the kitchen. Give them little jobs, conversing together as you work. Even these options may not be feasible if you're working overtime or hold two jobs. High-quality day care, where providers offer plenty of back-and-forth interchange and encourage kids to talk to one another, can help. Research shows children learn language from interactions with people, not from watching TV.

OLDER CHILDREN

Look for chances to talk with your children as they get older. A long drive to visit friends or relatives is a perfect time for you and the kids to tell jokes, laugh a lot, and play games. I always found car rides a relaxed time to ask my sons, "Where should we go on vacation next summer?" Or "How do you feel about tennis camp?" Because we know our children so well, we may assume we know what they think and feel. But often we don't know until we ask.

Make the dinner table a place to encourage your children to have opinions. Ask whether they think the family should get a cat, for example. Ask kids what they think about a TV news report or a candidate running for office. This sends the message that their views are valuable. There are some parents who ask their children to talk about a different topic every day. Not all of us want to go that far, but expressing opinions can be woven naturally into the family give-and-take. This is also a time to practice rules of listening, such as no interrupting, as well as table manners.

Turn the TV off in the kitchen at meals, but use TV as a conversation tool at other times. Watch programs together as much as possible, and be aware of issues they raise. Segue into topics you can discuss. You might ask your youngster, "What do you think about the decision [name of TV character] made?" or "How would you respond in that situation?"

Teach youngsters how to greet Aunt Milly and Uncle Louie when you all go to their house for Christmas dinner—how to say hello, and later good-bye and thank you. Knowledge of proper etiquette gives kids confidence and is a lifelong strength.

Encourage children to interact with adults at gatherings of friends and family. That's how they gain experience in talking to various types of people, and get comfortable in social situations. I've always admired a friend's children, who range in age from elementary school to college. At our periodic women's poker games, the kids have always been allowed to chat with us. We want to know all about their news and they love telling us. They feel at ease around adults because their parents provide them with plenty of practice.

TEENS

One of the best ways to help teens improve conversation skills is to prep them before they attend an occasion where adults will ask, "How's school?" or "Where do you want to go to college?" or "Play any sports?" Your child can practice answers in advance to help overcome initial awkwardness.

Encourage teens to ask their own questions, too. For example, teens tend to be interested in the work adults do, and grown-ups like talking about their jobs. If the youngster will attend a wedding or other event where a lawyer or a baker will be present, he/she can prepare some questions to ask, such as, "Do bakers really have to get up at three a.m.?" At the same time, point out that questions like "How much money do you make?" are not appropriate. Learning this kind of social savvy will be invaluable throughout life.

Years ago it was thought that children should be seen and not heard. Yet we now know that talking to children and showing them how to respond has a huge positive impact on so many areas of their development, including their verbal abilities. Take small steps, enlist cooperation, and be a cheerleader who celebrates your child's efforts. Always incorporate fun in your interactions. That's how children learn.

(14)

START TALKING

"My conversation skills go out the window when I walk into a room full of people. I freeze and all these fears rise up. 'I'm overweight. No one will want to talk to me. They're together; they're friends. Why would they want to know me?' I know it's irrational, but I feel awkward and I project it. It's hard to listen. I was a misfit as a kid and people made fun of me." This statement comes from a friend of mine who is smart, talented, and very funny. It took her years to get comfortable talking to people after religious services. Yet she did. Someone else could not make eye contact. Through sheer force of will, he finally started looking directly at people he was talking to.

Is it easy to accomplish change? No. But you can help hasten the process.

One way is to practice new skills now. Before the next invitation to a cocktail party, dinner, or symposium arrives in the mail, start noticing people around you and try to talk to everyone. Smile and say hello in the elevator. If the weather outside is frigid and someone is lightly dressed, make a comment like "You're brave in this weather." People usually respond to such chitchat and it's a way to loosen up and rehearse. Talk to people on line at the dry cleaner or the Starbucks kiosk. Talk to someone on the next treadmill at the health club, at your place of worship, or while walking the dog. There are lots of opportunities to talk on the street *except when* you have a phone or iPod stuck in your ear. Ask directions or offer them to someone who looks lost. It's the friendly thing to do, and it will help you become more relaxed with conversation. Look around for inspiration and you'll find things to talk about. You never know where you'll meet a client, customer, or contact or learn something new.

THE NEXT STEPS

There are times, however, when you may want or need more than this book. Perhaps you aren't achieving what you want to achieve or you want extra help with specific skills. There are many resources available today.

Books and Classes

A banker told me, "People do forget their manners and are sometimes oblivious to how they come across. I was at a business lunch, and a guy was shoveling food into his mouth. If I'm thinking of working with someone, part of my job is to assess the person's skill set, and table manners are part of sophistication and savvy. This is about nuances, and insensitivity to what's going on. This guy was also very rude to the waitress, which is telling. If that's how he relates to a third party, what does that mean to people who deal with him?"

Conversation skills don't exist in a vacuum. The impression you make also depends on behavior, body language, and a variety of other factors. Books on etiquette, including international etiquette, are full of good advice. Keep one or more on your shelf for easy referral or check out etiquette books from the library. In this coarsened American culture, many people haven't learned the basics of good manners. Yet you're expected to know them, especially as you advance in your career. You can't wait for someone else to tell you what's appropriate. (Few people will.) It's your responsibility to learn.

Classes on manners, dining skills, and international etiquette and protocol are available at places like the Protocol School of Washington (www.psow.com) and the Charleston School of Protocol and Etiquette (www.charlestonschoolof protocol.com). Check out these and other classes, including local ones, online or in the yellow pages. The International School of Protocol (www.internationalschoolofprotocol.com) also offers courses on effective listening, and the American Management Association (www.amanet.org) offers seminars on listening skills.

Personal Coaches

Coaching is a relatively new field that has emerged as a result of changes in our society and in the world. Coaches have become popular resources for support and feedback as job security has all but disappeared, and entrepreneurship has sky-rocketed. A coach is a professional who partners with you to help maximize your personal and professional growth potential, according to the International Coach Federation (ICF), a global association of personal and business coaches.

A coach may be useful when you face new challenges or opportunities where you have to stretch. Perhaps you're moving from middle to senior management. The way you conduct yourself is a huge factor in whether you're accepted, and a coach can help you develop the poise, presence, and savvy to fit into your new role. Some chief executives turn to coaches to polish rough edges and become more cultivated.

Or you may want to improve faster than you can by yourself. Coaches who specialize in particular areas can help. For example, if you're job hunting and have had many interviews but no offers, you may benefit from a professional diagnosis by a career coach or interview coach to figure out what went wrong and how to proceed in the future. Dating coaches can assess your romantic strengths and weaknesses and help you connect.

Voice and dialect coaches can make a difference, too. Tone, volume, and other factors count—in everyday conversations, meetings, presentations, and on the phone. Arnold Schwarzenegger took voice lessons years ago, and I once went to a coach to tone down my Brooklyn accent. Many professionals and business executives for whom English is a second language turn to voice coaches for "accent reduction."

Coaching can take place in person, on the phone, or sometimes online, and might run for three to six months for a very specific problem or for a longer period. Rates may range anywhere from $60 to $250 per hour or more. In some instances, your company may be willing to pay the fee. The ICF (www.coachfederation.org) certifies coaches, accredits coaching schools, and offers a coach referral service. You can also check the International Association of Coaching (IAC) at www.certifiedcoach.org, the Association for Coaching (AC) at www.associationforcoaching.com, and the Worldwide Association of Business Coaches at www.wabccoaches.com.

Mental-Health Professionals

Some people are more than just shy. They suffer from social anxiety disorder (or social phobia), which affects about 15 million adult men and women in the United States and can be disabling without treatment. The disorder can involve a single situation, such as chatting with people, or life in general. Symptoms include intense chronic fear of being watched and judged by others and of feeling humiliated by saying or doing the wrong thing. Excessive sweating, blushing, trembling, and nausea may be physical manifestations. If social anxiety interferes with your functioning in daily life, cognitive behavior therapy (and sometimes medications) can help. Talk to your family physician about whether a referral to a psychotherapist specializing in social anxiety is appropriate.

For additional information on social anxiety and on locating mental-health services in your area, see the National Institute of Mental Health (NIMH) Web site at www.nimh.nih.gov/health/publications/anxiety-disorders.

BE YOUR BEST

Don't let your insecurities hold you back. We all feel anxious and doubt ourselves at times. We all want to feel safe and comfortable; we don't like being vulnerable. Almost half of us consider ourselves shy. Yet many people, including some famous stutterers like Jack Welch, former CEO of General Electric; Tiger Woods; and even Winston Churchill overcame their difficulties to become successful at talking to people.

It is possible to change the movie in your mind and picture yourself the way you are now. You aren't at camp or at school anymore. You're a grown-up at a social or business event, and you have tools at your disposal. As you master new skills and refuse to let fear of rejection immobilize you, you can begin to experience situations differently and behave differently. Such changes do require frequent self-talk and the ability to give yourself credit for what you *can* do. If you're fine one-on-one at small dinners, maybe your script is "I can build on that at a cocktail party, even if more people are around."

As you replace the habit of "I can't" with "I can try," you'll meet lots of people, enjoy small moments, and sometimes make new friends. The challenge is to put your best self forward. You can become a better conversationalist if you're willing to practice the skills you've learned in this book. I know you can.